DELICIOUS AF
Vegan

100
Simple Recipes for
Wildly Flavorful Plant-Based
Comfort Foods

Lauren Boehme
Author of *Southern Vegan*

PAGE STREET
PUBLISHING CO.

Dedication

For Lenore, because she is the reason I do anything.
For Terry, because I love him more than food, and I love food an awful lot.
For Julie, because a better person doesn't exist.

PAGE STREET
PUBLISHING CO.

Copyright © 2023 Lauren Boehme and Julie Grace

First published in 2023 by
Page Street Publishing Co.
27 Congress Street, Suite 1511
Salem, MA 01970
www.pagestreetpublishing.com

Distributed by Macmillan, sales in Canada by The Canadian Manda Group.

27 26 25 24 23   1 2 3 4 5

ISBN-13: 978-1-64567-934-9
ISBN-10: 1-64567-934-9

Library of Congress Control Number: 2022949672

Cover and book design by Meg Baskis for Page Street Publishing Co.
Photography by Lauren Boehme and Julie Grace

Printed and bound in China

Contents

Introduction

What is comfort food to you? Is it just a sweet or a hearty recipe? Is it a dish that reminds you of a Sunday night meal with your whole family when you were 9 years old?

I believe comfort food is a dish that makes you feel warm and cozy on a cold evening. It's an occasional indulgent dessert just because the flavor makes you feel alive and joyful. It's a recipe that you want to share with your daughter, because it was your absolute favorite thing when you were her age. Comfort food brings a smile to your face. It makes your heart feel warm. It celebrates life. It just makes you *feel good*.

The goal of my blog, Rabbit and Wolves, and this cookbook is to prove that incorporating more plant-based food into your life doesn't mean you should give up on the flavors you know and love or the joy of eating. Eating should be fun, be filled with pleasure and bring us all together. Vegan comfort food allows me to enjoy the plant-based version of my favorite childhood foods, without participating in the harming of animals. It's eating delicious treats minus the cruelty.

If you read my first cookbook, *Southern Vegan*, you know that I stopped eating meat when I was 12 years old, after a school project left me reeling about meat industry practices. These practices have only gotten more earth-destructive and inhumane. Veganism isn't going anywhere. More and more people are turning to part-time or full-time plant-based living. Fast food companies now have plant-based burgers and nuggets on their menus, and local restaurant favorites are adding more vegan/vegetarian fare. My goal is never to convince anyone to go vegan. We all have our own values and life circumstances. I don't expect everyone to think or act exactly as I do.

One of the things I love most about being a vegan recipe developer and chef is the challenge of taking some of my most-loved childhood favorites and turning them into plant-based delectable delights. In culinary school, I was told that I would never get anywhere in my field if I didn't eat meat. So naturally, after receiving my culinary arts degree, I made it my mission to create vegan food that everyone could enjoy, vegan or not. My food blog, Rabbit and Wolves, has become popular because it features food that entire families can enjoy. You certainly don't have to be a full-time vegan to enjoy this cookbook.

While this is, in fact, a plant-based cookbook, the theme truly is *warm-you-right-up good food*. Even the most cold-hearted human can be turned warm (if only for a few moments) by a dish that reminds them of their beloved grandmother. It's true!

I've included some of my favorite one-pot wonders for those hectic weeknights when you need to get dinner on the table in a hurry. You'll also find recipes that will impress your guests at celebratory feasts, your summer barbecue or birthday parties. Don't forget the sweet treats. I love a decadent dessert. No matter which chapter you find yourself in, you can rest assured that you'll be diving into a vegan dish that is fun, tasty and classically comforting. So, turn the page and begin your exciting journey into delicious and cozy vegan fare.

Indulgent MORNINGS

Picture it: Venice (Florida) 1993. It's Monday morning, and I throw a waffle in the toaster and slather it with smooth peanut butter. Then I proceed to heat my peanut butter waffle in the microwave for exactly 20 seconds. No more, no less. Twenty seconds was the sweet spot. Tuesday, same thing. Wednesday, well, you get the idea. I ate so many frozen waffles that year, I should have bought stock. I unfortunately didn't have that foresight, because I was 9 years old, and no money manager would take me on as a client.

Thankfully, my palate has become more refined with age. We work hard, we raise families, we deal with adult life every day. We deserve more than frozen peanut butter waffles, gosh darn it. These indulgent vegan recipes are all based on childhood favorites, but they are, by and large, way more lavish and delicious. Pinky-in-the-air fancy. The scratch-made Churro Bagels with Sweet Vanilla Cream Cheeze (page 12) are absolutely heavenly. The Blueberry Pancake Pop Tarts (page 17) are a unique combination of two of my first loves. The Vanilla Bean Spiced Apple Fritters (page 23) are a nod to those carefree childhood weekends. Swanky "Sausage," "Egg" and Cheeze Breakfast Sandwiches (page 18) prove even a drive-through staple can be high-tea worthy. In this chapter, you will inevitably find your new motivation to hop right out of bed on Saturday morning (though some of these recipes are perfect for brunch, as they require a bit more time to prepare). Get ready to be that person that yells "Heck yes!" in someone's face when they ask, "Are you a morning person?"

Chai Latte Crepes

Have you ever wanted to eat a chai latte? This recipe is for you. Not only will you be diving into a delicious chai-spiced crepe, but you'll also enjoy a fluffy and decadent chai-spiced whipped cream. Double chai? Um, yes please. To achieve the fluffiness without the standard egg, you'll use sparkling water. Throw some fresh berries in and you've got yourself a delicious and particularly lavish breakfast. Feel free to take photos to share on Instagram to show everyone how elegant you are.

Serves 6

Chai-Spiced Whipped Cream
1 cup (240 ml) vegan whipping cream (I prefer Silk®)

⅓ cup (40 g) vegan confectioners' sugar

¼ tsp ground cinnamon

¼ tsp cardamom

Pinch of nutmeg

Pinch of cloves

Pinch of ground ginger

Pinch of allspice

Pinch of salt

½ tsp vanilla extract

Chai-Spiced Crepes
1½ cups (185 g) all-purpose flour

1 tbsp (8 g) cornstarch

1 tsp ground cinnamon

½ tsp ground ginger

½ tsp cardamom

½ tsp allspice

¼ tsp nutmeg

¼ tsp cloves

1 tbsp (13 g) organic cane sugar

½ tsp salt

Pinch of black pepper

2 tbsp (28 g) vegan butter, melted, plus extra for the pan (I prefer Earth Balance®)

1 cup (240 ml) oat milk or other nondairy milk

1 cup (240 ml) sparkling water (or regular)

Fresh berries, for the inside of the crepes (optional)

Make the chai-spiced whipped cream. In a large mixing bowl or the bowl of a stand mixer, whip the whipping cream until it starts to thicken. Add the confectioners' sugar, cinnamon, cardamom, nutmeg, cloves, ginger, allspice and salt. Continue whipping until the cream starts to get really thick. Add the vanilla, and continue to whip until the cream forms stiff peaks. Put the whipped cream in the refrigerator while you make the crepes.

Make the crepes. In a large mixing bowl, sift together the flour, cornstarch, cinnamon, ginger, cardamom, allspice, nutmeg and cloves. Stir in the sugar, salt and pepper. Add 2 tablespoons (28 g) of the butter, the milk and water to the mixing bowl, and whisk until you have a completely smooth batter.

In a large nonstick skillet over medium-high heat, heat about 1 tablespoon (14 g) of the butter. Once the butter is melted, add about ⅓ cup (120 ml) of the crepe batter to the skillet. Immediately swirl it around the pan to make one very thin circle. Cook the crepe for 2 to 3 minutes on the first side; it will start to cook through the other side and will begin to look firm. Slide a thin metal spatula under the crepe, and carefully flip the crepe. Cook for another 2 to 3 minutes, or until the crepe is cooked through. Take the crepe out of the pan, and put it on a plate. Repeat with the remaining crepe batter.

Once the crepes are ready, fill a crepe with a little bit of the chai-spiced whipped cream and some berries, if desired. Roll the crepe up, and top with a bit more whipped cream. Serve immediately.

Liège Waffles with Berry Compote

These waffles, made with yeast dough, will honestly blow your mind. If you've never heard of liège waffles, think of them as a perfect puffy cinnamon roll but in waffle form. You'll also be adding pearl sugar (compressed sugar clumps that add a crunchy pop of sweetness) to the dough, which creates amazing little pockets of caramelized sugar during the cooking process. When the waffles are done, pour some warm berry compote on top and add some vegan whipped cream if you like. If you think that these waffles sound incredible, you are absolutely right.

Yields 10 waffles

Liège Waffles

¾ cup (180 ml) warm nondairy milk (about 110°F [43°C])

2 tsp (6 g) active dry yeast

2 tbsp (26 g) organic cane sugar

½ cup (120 ml) applesauce

2 tsp (10 ml) vanilla extract

12 tbsp (168 g) vegan butter, melted and slightly cooled

1 tsp salt

3½ cups (438 g) all-purpose flour, plus more for dusting

8 oz (227 g) Belgian pearl sugar (beet sugar)

Berry Compote

3 cups (450 g) fresh or frozen berries (such as blueberries, strawberries and raspberries)

3 tbsp (45 ml) orange juice

1 tsp organic cane sugar

Vegan whipped cream, for serving (optional)

Make the waffle dough first. In a large mixing bowl or the bowl of a stand mixer fitted with the dough hook, add the warm milk. Sprinkle the yeast over the milk, then sprinkle the cane sugar over the yeast. Stir with a spoon, and then let it sit for about 5 minutes. The yeast should bloom and get bubbly and frothy.

Add the applesauce, vanilla and butter to the bowl with the milk mixture, and stir with a rubber spatula or the dough hook (if you are using a stand mixer). Add the salt and stir. Add the flour about 1 cup (125 g) at a time, and stir or knead with the dough hook until the mixture forms a smooth ball. Knead for another 1 to 2 minutes. Add a bit more flour if the mixture is still sticky.

Put the dough in a bowl sprayed with nonstick spray, cover it with a kitchen towel and proof it in a warm, dry place for about 30 minutes.

While the dough proofs, make the compote. In a medium saucepan, stir together the berries, orange juice and cane sugar. Heat the saucepan over medium heat, and bring the berry mixture to a simmer. Reduce the heat to medium-low, and simmer for 10 to 12 minutes. Let the compote cool while you finish the waffles.

After the dough has proofed, sprinkle the pearl sugar over the dough, and fold the pearl sugar into the dough. Turn the dough out onto a floured surface, and continue kneading, making sure the pearl sugar is evenly distributed. Divide the dough into about 10 pieces, and roll each piece into a ball. Let the dough rise again for 5 to 7 minutes while you preheat the waffle maker.

Spray the waffle maker with nonstick spray. Then place one of the waffle dough balls directly in the center of the waffle maker. Close the waffle maker, and cook the waffles for 5 to 7 minutes, or until cooked through. Repeat with the remaining waffle dough.

Serve immediately with the berry compote and vegan whipped cream, if desired.

*See image on page 8.

Autumn Pear Baked French Toast

This recipe is for all you pumpkin spice latte–drinking, cozy sweater–cuddling, pumpkin patch–going, fall-loving human beings out there. This French toast checks off all the most-loved flavors of fall and makes your house smell like a Yankee candle from the mall downtown. The nice mall. You know which one. Bake the pecan French toast, then pour the delicious spiced caramelized pear syrup over top. Serve with a dollop of vegan whipped cream and die from contentedness.

Serves 6

Pecan Baked French Toast

2 cups (250 g) roasted, salted pecans, divided

2 cups (480 ml) nondairy milk

⅓ cup (80 ml) maple syrup

1 tbsp (15 ml) vanilla extract

¼ cup (31 g) all-purpose flour

1 tsp ground cinnamon

¼ tsp salt

1 loaf (16 oz) vegan bread (I prefer vegan brioche from Trader Joe's®)

Spiced Caramelized Pear Syrup

5 small or 4 medium Bartlett pears, diced (about 2½ cups [400 g])

½ tsp cardamom

½ tsp ground cinnamon

Pinch of cloves

3 tbsp (43 g) vegan butter

⅓ cup (73 g) vegan light brown sugar

1 tsp vanilla extract

Pinch of salt

Vegan whipped cream, for topping (optional)

Preheat the oven to 350°F (176°C).

Make pecan butter. Add 1 cup (125 g) of the pecans to a food processor, and process until you have a fairly smooth pecan butter. It may take 4 to 5 minutes, depending on your food processor. Scrape down the sides as needed. You should end up with ½ cup (130 g) of pecan butter. Roughly chop and sprinkle the remaining 1 cup (125 g) of pecans evenly in the bottom of a 7 x 11–inch (18 x 28–cm) baking dish.

Make the custard. In a large mixing bowl, whisk together the pecan butter, milk, maple syrup, vanilla, flour, cinnamon and salt. Whisk until completely smooth.

Dip each slice of bread into the custard mixture on each side, and let the bread soak in a lot of the mixture. Layer the slices of bread in the baking dish at a slight angle in two rows, so they will all fit. Drizzle the remaining custard mixture over the bread, and bake for 43 to 45 minutes. The custard should be thick and the bread should look firm.

While the French toast bakes, make the spiced caramelized pear syrup. In a small mixing bowl, toss the pears with the cardamom, cinnamon and cloves. In a small saucepan over medium heat, heat the butter. Once the butter is melted, add the brown sugar, vanilla and salt. Whisk to combine. Simmer over medium-low heat until the brown sugar dissolves, 2 to 3 minutes. Add the spiced pears, and stir to combine. Bring to a simmer, then let the pears simmer for 10 to 15 minutes, or until they are nice and soft. Turn off the heat.

Once the French toast is done, served topped with the spiced caramelized pear syrup and vegan whipped cream, if desired.

*See image on page 8.

Churro Bagels with Sweet Vanilla Cream Cheeze

I enrolled in cosmetology school straight out of high school, and during that year, almost every morning for breakfast I ate a vegan cinnamon crunch bagel with cream cheese. While that might not be a great breakfast to have on a daily basis, I still look back on that time in my life fondly. So I created these churro bagels for you to combine two of my longtime favorite things. These bagels, made from scratch, are soft and chewy, and that oh-so-crunchy churro topping is hard to beat. The sweet vanilla cream cheeze was born to go with these bagels. They take time to prepare, but I promise it's worth it: eat one of these babies fresh out of the oven, and your life will be forever changed.

Yields 10 bagels

Churro Bagels
2 cups (480 ml) warm water (about 110°F [43°C])

4½ tsp (14 g) active dry yeast

2 tbsp (26 g) organic cane sugar

5 cups (625 g) all-purpose flour, plus more for dusting

1 tbsp (8 g) ground cinnamon

1 tbsp (14 g) vegan light brown sugar

1 tsp salt

Dusting
¼ cup (51 g) organic cane sugar

2 tsp (5 g) ground cinnamon

¼ cup (54 g) vegan butter, melted

Make the dough. Pour the warm water into the bowl of a stand mixer or a large mixing bowl. Sprinkle the yeast into the water, and sprinkle the cane sugar over the yeast. Let the yeast bloom for 5 to 6 minutes. The yeast should puff up and be bubbly.

In a separate large mixing bowl, sift together the flour and cinnamon, then stir in the brown sugar and salt. Start adding the dry ingredients to the bowl with the water and yeast, a little at a time. If you are using a stand mixer, use the dough hook to combine and begin to knead. Once all the dry ingredients are incorporated, continue to knead the dough for 2 to 3 minutes. The dough should come together in a ball and no longer be sticky. If you aren't using a stand mixer, begin stirring in the dry ingredients by hand, and then knead by hand when it gets too difficult to stir. Knead by hand for 2 to 3 minutes, or until the dough forms a ball and is no longer sticky.

Remove the dough from the bowl and grease the bowl, either with nonstick spray or by brushing it with a little bit of oil. Return the dough to the bowl. Cover the dough with a kitchen towel, and place it in a warm, dry place. Let it proof for 1 to 1½ hours. The dough will double in size. (I like to preheat my oven to 250°F [121°C], then turn the oven off and let the dough rise in the warm oven.)

While the dough proofs, make the dusting for the bagels. In a small mixing bowl, mix together the cane sugar and cinnamon. Set aside.

(continued)

Churro Bagels with Sweet Vanilla Cream Cheeze (Continued)

Topping

¾ cup (153 g) organic cane sugar

1 tbsp (8 g) ground cinnamon

2 tbsp (28 g) room-temperature vegan butter

Sweet Vanilla Cream Cheeze

8 oz (226 g) vegan cream cheese

¼ cup (30 g) vegan confectioners' sugar

2 tsp (10 ml) vanilla extract

Make the topping. In a small mixing bowl, stir together the cane sugar and cinnamon. Then add the butter to the bowl and, using a fork or your fingers, press and push the butter into the sugar and cinnamon until it resembles a crumble texture. Set aside.

Once the dough has risen, punch the dough down in the center, then turn the dough out onto a floured surface. Cut it into about 10 equal portions. Roll each piece into a ball. Push your thumb through the center of the ball to create the hole for the bagel. Make the hole a little bit bigger by working your thumb around the hole. Place each bagel on a large baking sheet that is lined with parchment paper or a silicone mat. Cover the bagels with a kitchen towel, and let them rise for another 15 minutes.

Preheat the oven to 425°F (218°C).

Bring a large pot of water to a boil. Reduce the heat to medium so the water is at a soft boil. Add two to three bagels at a time to the boiling water, and boil for 2 minutes. Flip the bagels, and boil for another 2 minutes. Remove from the water with a large slotted spoon. Place each bagel back on the baking sheet, and repeat with all of the bagels.

Brush the bagels with the melted butter for the dusting, and then generously dust/sprinkle the top of the bagels with the cinnamon-sugar mixture. Sprinkle the crumbly topping evenly on top of each of the bagels. Bake the bagels for 25 to 27 minutes, or until golden brown. Let the bagels cool completely; the topping will get nice and crunchy.

While the bagels cool, make the cream cheeze. In a large mixing bowl or the bowl of a stand mixer, add the cream cheese. Using the whisk attachment for the stand mixer or a hand mixer, whip the cream cheese for 1 to 2 minutes. Add the confectioners' sugar and vanilla, and continue to whip until everything is fully combined. Put the cream cheeze in the refrigerator until ready to use.

Slice the bagels, and serve smeared with the sweet vanilla cream cheeze. If you aren't eating the bagels immediately, I recommend reheating them for about 30 seconds in the microwave.

Store the leftover bagels in a ziplock bag for 3 to 4 days. Store the cream cheeze in an airtight container in the refrigerator for up to a week.

Chick'n and Red Velvet Waffles

Say hello to your new favorite brunch treat! I adore red velvet *anything*, and I can also get down on "chicken" and waffles regularly, so I combined the two. These waffles are crispy on the outside and moist and fluffy on the inside. The "chicken," made from tofu, is crunchy and savory. Pour on the maple syrup, and go to town. Each bite is a sweet and savory dream.

Serves 6

Chick'n

1 (15-oz [425-g]) block extra-firm tofu, drained and pressed

2 tbsp (30 ml) extra-virgin olive oil

⅔ cup (160 ml) vegetable broth

¼ cup (60 ml) soy sauce

1 cup (120 g) vital wheat gluten

2⅓ cups (130 g) panko bread-crumbs, divided

1 tsp vegan chicken seasoning or bouillon

A few pinches of salt and pepper

Extra-virgin olive oil, for brushing

Red Velvet Waffles

2 cups (250 g) all-purpose flour

1½ tbsp (21 g) baking powder

3 tbsp (16 g) cocoa powder

⅓ cup (67 g) organic cane sugar

½ tsp salt

1¾ cups (420 ml) almond milk

2½ tsp (13 ml) apple cider vinegar

⅓ cup (72 g) vegan butter, melted

½ cup (120 ml) applesauce

2 tsp (10 ml) vanilla extract

2 tbsp (30 ml) vegan red food coloring

Maple syrup, for topping

Preheat the oven to 425°F (218°C).

Start the chick'n. In a food processor, crumble in the tofu. Add the olive oil, broth, soy sauce, wheat gluten, 1⅓ cups (74 g) of the panko bread-crumbs, chicken seasoning and a few pinches of salt and pepper. Pulse, scraping down the sides as needed, until the mixture comes together and forms a dough ball. The mixture should be stretchy. Form chick'n pieces out of the dough ball by taking about ¼ cup (60 g) of the mixture and forming it into a chicken tender shape. Repeat with all of the dough.

In a medium mixing bowl, combine the remaining 1 cup (56 g) of panko breadcrumbs and a pinch of salt and pepper. Put one of the chick'n tenders into the panko breadcrumbs, and press the breadcrumbs onto the outside of the chick'n. Repeat with all the chick'n.

Put the chick'n on a baking sheet sprayed with nonstick spray or brushed with olive oil. Brush the tops of the chick'n with more olive oil. Bake the chick'n for 15 minutes, flip, and bake for another 17 to 22 minutes, or until the chick'n is crunchy on the outside and firm on the inside. It will puff up a bit, but as it cools the texture will firm.

While the chick'n bakes, make the waffles. In a large mixing bowl, sift the flour, baking powder and cocoa powder. Stir in the sugar and salt. Set aside.

In a small mixing bowl, whisk together the almond milk and apple cider vinegar. Let it sit for 2 to 3 minutes. It will curdle slightly. Pour the almond milk mixture into the dry ingredients. Pour in the butter, applesauce, vanilla and food coloring. Whisk until the mixture is fully combined and smooth.

Heat a waffle iron on medium-high. Spray the waffle iron with nonstick spray, and fill the center of the waffle iron with ⅓ to ½ cup (80 to 120 ml) of the batter. Cook for 2 to 3 minutes. The waffle iron will usually indicate when the waffle is ready. Repeat with all of the batter.

Once the chick'n is done, serve on top of the waffles, drizzled with maple syrup.

*See photo on page 6.

Blueberry Pancake Pop Tarts®

These blueberry pop tarts® are a treat for breakfast or any time of day. A flaky, buttery pastry filled with blueberry pie filling topped with a sweet maple icing. If you're asking yourself, "Should I try this recipe?" the answer is a resounding *yes*.

Yields 6 pastries

Blueberry Filling

2 tbsp (16 g) cornstarch

⅓ cup (67 g) organic cane sugar

½ cup (120 ml) water

2 cups (296 g) fresh blueberries

1 tsp lemon juice

Pop Tart Crust

3 cups (375 g) all-purpose flour, plus more for dusting

1 tbsp (13 g) organic cane sugar

½ tsp salt

½ cup (108 g) cold vegan butter

½ cup (95 g) vegetable shortening

½ cup (120 ml) cold water

Maple Frosting

2 cups (240 g) vegan confectioners' sugar

2 tbsp (30 ml) maple syrup

1 tbsp (15 ml) nondairy milk, plus more as needed

Pinch of salt

Dried blueberries, crushed, for topping (optional)

Make the filling. In a medium saucepan, whisk together the cornstarch and cane sugar. Pour in the water, and whisk to combine, making sure there are no lumps of cornstarch.

Add the blueberries and lemon juice. Stir to combine. Heat the saucepan over medium heat. Bring the mixture to a simmer, reduce the heat to medium-low and let it simmer, stirring frequently, until the blueberries burst and the mixture starts to thicken, 7 to 9 minutes. Let the mixture cool. It will thicken more as it cools.

While the filling cools, make the crust. In a food processor, add the flour, cane sugar and salt. Pulse to combine. Cut the butter into small chunks, and break apart the vegetable shortening into chunks. Drop the chunks of butter and shortening into the food processor on top of the dry ingredients. Pulse a few times to evenly combine everything. The mixture should resemble sand.

With the food processor running, drizzle in the cold water. Process until the dough comes together and forms a ball. Chill the dough if not using immediately.

When you're ready to make the pop tarts, preheat the oven to 350°F (176°C). Line a baking sheet with parchment paper.

On a floured work surface, roll the dough into a large rectangle. You want it to be pretty thin, about ⅛ inch (3 mm) thick. Cut about 12 equal rectangles out of the dough. Fill the center of 6 of the rectangles with about a table-spoon (15 ml) of the blueberry filling. Place another rectangle of dough on top of the blueberry filling. Repeat with all of the dough. Press the prongs of a fork down around the edges of each pop tart to seal them.

Place all the pop tarts on the prepared baking sheet. Bake them for 15 to 17 minutes, or until the pop tarts are golden brown and the dough is crisp on the outside.

While the pop tarts bake, make the maple frosting. In a medium mixing bowl, whisk together the confectioners' sugar, maple syrup, milk and salt. You want the frosting to be pretty thick so it stays on the pop tart. If it's too thick to drizzle, add a splash more milk.

Once the pop tarts are done, let them cool. Then frost the tops and sprinkle with crushed dried blueberries, if desired. The pastries can be stored in the refrigerator for 4 to 5 days and reheated in a toaster oven.

Swanky "Sausage," "Egg" and Cheeze Breakfast Sandwiches

I *love* breakfast sandwiches. So naturally I had to share one of my favorite breakfast sandwich recipes with you beautiful people. We've got the classic "sausage, egg and cheese" elements to please our taste buds, but when we add the sun-dried tomato aioli . . . well, I'll just let you see for yourself. I'll give you a hint: the sun-dried tomato aioli is *bomb*. If you're a breakfast sandwich fanatic like myself, this recipe will be on your regular rotation. It deserves nothing less.

Serves 4

Sun-Dried Tomato Aioli

½ cup (120 ml) vegan mayonnaise

¼ cup (14 g) sun-dried tomatoes, roughly chopped

2 cloves garlic, grated

Pinch of salt

Pinch of cayenne

Sandwiches

4 frozen hashbrowns

2 tbsp (30 ml) extra-virgin olive oil, plus more as needed

4 vegan breakfast sausages

12 oz (355 ml) vegan egg

Salt and pepper, to taste

4 slices vegan Cheddar-style cheese

4 vegan bagels (such as everything bagels)

1 cup (20 g) arugula

Make the sun-dried tomato aioli. In a small mixing bowl, whisk together the mayonnaise, sun-dried tomatoes, garlic and a pinch each of salt and cayenne. Put the aioli in the refrigerator until ready to use.

Make the sandwiches. Begin by baking the hashbrowns according to the package directions.

Next, cook the sausages. In a large nonstick skillet over medium-high heat, heat the olive oil. Sauté the sausages for 2 to 3 minutes per side or until golden brown. Remove the sausages.

In the same pan, add a little more olive oil if needed, and pour the egg into the pan, spreading the mixture out evenly. Season with a few pinches of salt and pepper. Continue to cook until the underside is done and bubbles start to come through the top, 2 to 3 minutes. Divide the egg into four equal portions, then flip and continue to cook them until they are completely done, 2 to 3 minutes, or until the egg is firm. Put a slice of Cheddar on top of each portion of eggs, and let it melt. You can cover the pan to help this process.

Toast the bagels, if desired, and once the hashbrowns, sausages and eggs are done, put together the sandwiches. Spread some of the sun-dried tomato aioli on each side of a bagel. Then put the egg and cheese on the bottom, top with a sausage patty and a hashbrown. Top that with a little more aioli and some arugula.

Repeat with the remaining ingredients to make four sandwiches, and serve immediately.

Ethan's Spicy Roja Chilaquiles

My brother Ethan loves chilaquiles. He is definitely a savory breakfast person, and he also has to eat gluten-free. Ethan was one of my inspirations for going vegetarian many moons ago. So, in honor of our shared journey, and also just because he is all around the best freaking person, I made a breakfast we could both have. Instead of eggs, I used vegan eggs, which cook up similarly to a regular scrambled egg. Refried beans, freshly fried tortilla strips and this roja sauce are incredible together.

Serves 4

Salsa Roja
1 lb (454 g) Roma tomatoes, diced

½ white onion, roughly chopped

1 jalapeño, deseeded and roughly chopped

2 cloves garlic

¼ cup (4 g) fresh cilantro

2 tsp (10 ml) lime juice

1 tbsp (15 ml) extra-virgin olive oil

Salt, to taste

Chips
¼ cup (60 ml) vegetable oil

12 corn tortillas, cut into 8 wedges

Salt, to taste

Toppings
1 (16-oz [454-g]) can vegetarian refried beans, heated

½ cup (120 ml) vegan eggs, cooked (I prefer Simply Eggless® or JUST Egg)

Guacamole and vegan sour cream (optional)

Make the salsa roja. In a blender, add the tomatoes, onion, jalapeño, garlic, cilantro and lime juice. Blend until smooth.

In a large nonstick skillet over medium heat, heat the olive oil. Pour the salsa roja into the skillet, and season with a few pinches of salt. Bring to a simmer, reduce the heat to low and simmer for 3 to 5 minutes. Taste and adjust the seasonings. Leave the heat on low while you make the rest.

Make the chips. In a small skillet over medium-high heat, heat the olive oil. Once the oil is hot enough, it will form small bubbles. Fry a handful of the tortilla wedges at a time until they are golden brown, 2 to 3 minutes, reducing the heat as needed. (You'll know the heat needs to be reduced if the oil starts to smoke and the chips are browning too quickly.) Repeat with all of the tortilla wedges. Place the chips on a paper towel when they are done, and sprinkle with a few pinches of salt.

Put the chips into the skillet with the salsa, and toss to coat them. Let them cook in the salsa for about 1 minute.

Either serve the chilaquiles right out of the skillet, or pour them onto a plate. Top with the refried beans, eggs, guacamole and sour cream, if desired. Serve immediately.

Ranchero Breakfast Taquitos

When given a choice, I want to devour every breakfast item all together in one yummy little package. When that craving strikes, I love to turn to these breakfast taquitos—a delicious ranchero sauce tossed with some vegan breakfast sausage, diced potatoes and tofu scramble, rolled into cute little tortilla blankets and baked instead of fried. These are an essential savory breakfast. You can even make them ahead, freeze them and warm them up when you are in the mood.

Yields 12 taquitos

Ranchero Sauce
½ yellow onion, roughly chopped

1 jalapeño, deseeded and roughly chopped

4 cloves garlic

1 (8-oz [226-g]) can diced tomatoes

½ cup (120 ml) vegetable broth

1 tsp ancho chili powder

1 tsp chipotle powder

½ tsp Mexican oregano

½ tsp cumin

¼ tsp cayenne pepper

1 tsp lime juice

Salt, to taste

1 tbsp (15 ml) extra-virgin olive oil

Taquitos
2 tbsp (30 ml) extra-virgin olive oil

1 large russet potato, diced very finely

Salt and pepper, to taste

½ block (about 8 oz [226 g]) extra-firm tofu, drained and pressed

1 tsp garlic powder

½ tsp turmeric

4 vegan breakfast sausage patties

10 to 12 small flour tortillas

Nonstick cooking spray

Preheat the oven to 400°F (204°C). Spray a baking sheet with nonstick spray.

Make the ranchero sauce. In a blender, add the onion, jalapeño, garlic, tomatoes, broth, chili powder, chipotle powder, oregano, cumin, cayenne, lime juice and a pinch of salt. Pulse until the sauce is pretty smooth but still has a little texture.

In a medium saucepan over medium heat, heat the olive oil. Pour in the sauce, and bring to a simmer. Let the sauce simmer for 5 to 6 minutes; it will thicken slightly. Turn off the heat, and let the sauce sit while you make the rest.

Make the filling for the taquitos. In a large nonstick skillet over medium-high heat, heat the olive oil. Add the potato, and season with a pinch of salt and pepper. Sauté the potato for about 10 minutes, or until it starts to soften. Scoot the potato to one side of the skillet, and let it continue to cook. Crumble the tofu, and add it to the other side of the skillet. Sprinkle the garlic powder, turmeric and a pinch of salt and pepper over the tofu. Toss to combine.

Let the potato and the tofu sauté until the potato is tender and the tofu is golden brown and firm, 7 to 8 minutes. Toss the potato and tofu scramble together, and move them to one side of the skillet.

Put the sausage patties on the other side of the skillet, and sauté until they are cooked through, about 5 minutes. Break the patties up into chunks with a wooden spoon, then toss the potato, tofu and sausage together. Pour about half of the sauce into the skillet with the potato mixture, and toss to combine everything. Turn off the heat.

Fill the tortillas. Take one tortilla, and fill the center with 2 to 3 tablespoons (20 to 30 g) of the filling you made. Roll the tortilla into a cigar shape, then place it seam side down on the prepared baking sheet. Repeat with the remaining ingredients.

Spray the tops of the taquitos with more nonstick spray. Bake for 15 to 20 minutes. Once they are golden brown and crispy, serve the taquitos with the extra ranchero sauce for dipping.

*See photo on page 20.

Vanilla Bean Spiced Apple Fritters

Ah, good ole apple fritters. As much as I would absolutely shove a dozen regular apple fritters straight into my face any day of the week, I made these extra special. With the addition of vanilla bean paste, ginger, nutmeg and cardamom, these are are dressed to impress and will do just that. The yeasted dough takes some time to prepare, so this recipe is perfect for a late Sunday brunch, when you can linger in the kitchen without worrying about schedules or morning commitments. I love breaking off the little pieces of the fritters and pretending I'm in a cabin in the woods (not the horror movie kind) in autumn, leaves falling all around. Just sitting there alone with my thoughts, dipping my fritter into the coffee, without a care in the world . . .

Yields 10 fritters

Dough
½ cup (120 ml) warm water (about 110°F [43°C])

1½ tbsp (14 g) active dry yeast

1 tbsp (13 g) organic cane sugar

2 cups (250 g) all-purpose flour, plus more as needed

½ tsp ground cinnamon

½ tsp ground ginger

¼ tsp nutmeg

¼ tsp cardamom

¼ tsp baking powder

¼ cup (55 g) vegan light brown sugar

1 tsp salt

2 tbsp (27 g) room-temperature coconut oil

¼ cup (60 ml) applesauce

1 tsp vanilla extract

½ tsp vanilla bean paste

Apple Filling
2 large apples, peeled and diced

¼ cup (51 g) organic cane sugar

1 tsp lemon zest

1 tbsp (9 g) all-purpose flour

2 tsp (5 g) ground cinnamon

Make the dough. In the bowl of a stand mixer, stir together the water, yeast and cane sugar. Let it sit for about 5 minutes, or until the mixture gets bubbly and frothy.

While the yeast blooms, in a large mixing bowl, sift together the flour, cinnamon, ginger, nutmeg, cardamon and baking powder. Stir the brown sugar and salt into the bowl. Set aside.

Once the yeast is ready, add the coconut oil, applesauce, vanilla and vanilla bean paste to the bowl, and stir with the dough hook. While the dough hook is still going, add the dry ingredients, about ½ cup (65 g) at a time, until it is fully incorporated. Let the dough hook continue to knead until the dough forms a smooth ball, then let the hook knead for about 2 more minutes. If the dough is still a little sticky, add about 1 tablespoon (8 g) more of flour.

Put the dough ball into a large greased bowl. Cover the bowl with a kitchen towel, and let the dough rise in a warm, dry place for 1½ to 2 hours, or until the dough has doubled in size.

While the dough rises, make the apple filling. In a small saucepan, stir together the apples, sugar and lemon zest. Heat the saucepan over medium-low, and stir constantly, reducing the heat as needed. Simmer the apples until the liquid has been released and has thickened, 5 to 7 minutes. Let the apples cool.

Once the dough has doubled in size, punch down the dough, and turn it out onto a floured surface. Roll the dough out to about a ⅓-inch (8-mm)-thick rectangle.

Stir 1 tablespoon (9 g) of the flour into the saucepan with the cooled apples, making sure the flour is evenly distributed. The mixture will be moist.

(continued)

Vanilla Bean Spiced Apple Fritters (Continued)

Icing

2 cups (240 g) vegan confectioners' sugar

¼ tsp ground cinnamon

¼ cup (60 ml) oat milk or other nondairy milk

¼ tsp vanilla extract

½ tsp vanilla bean paste

Pinch of salt

Vegetable oil, for frying

Spread the apple mixture on top of half of the dough evenly. Sprinkle the entire top of the dough with the cinnamon for the filling. Fold the half of the dough that doesn't have the apples on top over the other half, and press the dough down onto the apples.

Roll the dough back out, with the apples in the middle, to ⅓ to ½ inch (8 mm to 1.3 cm) thick. Cut the dough into ½-inch (1.3-cm) squares; I like to use a pizza cutter for this. Gather 8 to 10 of the squares of dough, and press them together to form one ball. Repeat with all of the dough.

Place each fritter on some parchment paper, and cover with a kitchen towel. Let them rise for about 30 minutes.

While the fritters rise, make the icing. In a medium mixing bowl, whisk together the confectioners' sugar, cinnamon, milk, vanilla, vanilla bean paste and salt. Whisk until completely smooth. Set aside.

When you're ready to fry the fritters, heat 2 to 3 inches (5 to 8 cm) of vegetable oil in a saucepan over medium-high heat. Once the oil is ready, it will form tiny bubbles. Working in batches, fry the fritters for 2 to 3 minutes per side or until they are nice and golden brown and cooked through. If the fritters start to brown too fast, reduce the heat. Transfer the cooked fritters to a cooling rack.

Once you have fried all the fritters, let them cool for a few minutes, and either drizzle them or dunk them in the icing.

Black Forest Cinnamon Rolls

While this may not *look* like a traditional black forest dessert, I assure you, the flavor holds true. They are perfectly warm, gooey and cinnamon-y. Now, add a delicious melted dark chocolate filling, a decadent cream cheeze icing and a sweet and tart cherry compote on top, and you've got yourself a gem of a splurge-tastic breakfast.

If you have guests staying with you over a weekend, I recommend showing off your above-and-beyond hosting skills with this recipe. Make the rolls the night before and bake when ready in the morning. You will absolutely wow them with these cinnamon rolls. Also, you know, life is short. Make dessert for breakfast.

Serves 6

Dough
1 cup (240 ml) warm nondairy milk (about 110°F [43°C])

6 tbsp (78 g) organic cane sugar, divided

1 tbsp (9 g) active dry yeast

5 tbsp (70 g) vegan butter, melted and slightly cooled

½ cup (120 ml) applesauce

1 tsp salt

4 cups (500 g) all-purpose flour, plus more for dusting

Filling
6 tbsp (84 g) room-temperature vegan butter

½ cup (110 g) vegan light brown sugar

2 tbsp (11 g) cocoa powder

1 tsp ground cinnamon

1 tsp vanilla extract

½ tsp salt

4 oz (113 g) vegan dark chocolate (chunks or chips)

Prep the dough first. In the bowl of a stand mixer fitted with the dough hook, stir together the milk, 2 tablespoons (26 g) of the cane sugar and the yeast. Let it sit for about 5 minutes, or until it gets bubbly and frothy. Add the remaining 4 tablespoons (52 g) of the cane sugar, the butter and applesauce to the bowl, and stir.

While the dough hook is still going, add the salt. Slowly add the flour about ½ cup (63 g) at a time, until it is fully incorporated. Continue mixing until the dough forms into a ball. Knead the dough for about 2 more minutes. If the dough is still sticky, add another tablespoon (9 g) or so of flour.

Place the dough ball into a greased bowl, and let the dough rise until it has doubled in size, 1½ to 2 hours. Place the dough in a warm, dry place; I like to cover it with a kitchen towel.

While the dough rises, make the filling. In a medium mixing bowl, whisk together the butter, brown sugar, cocoa powder, cinnamon, vanilla and salt. Whisk until smooth. Set aside.

Cherry Compote

1 lb (454 g) cherries, pitted

3 tbsp (39 g) organic cane sugar

¼ cup (60 ml) cherry, grape or pomegranate juice

Pinch of salt

Icing

8 oz (226 g) room-temperature vegan cream cheese

½ cup (108 g) room-temperature vegan butter

1 tsp vanilla extract

Pinch of salt

3½ cups (420 g) vegan confectioners' sugar

Make the compote. In a medium saucepan, stir together the cherries, cane sugar, cherry juice and salt. Heat the saucepan over medium heat, and bring to a simmer. Reduce the heat to medium-low, and let the mixture simmer for 10 to 15 minutes, or until the juice has thickened slightly and the cherries are soft. Set aside and let it cool.

Once the dough has risen, punch it down, and turn it out onto a floured surface. Roll the dough out with a rolling pin to a ⅓- to ½-inch (8-mm to 1.3-cm) thickness and about a 12-inch (30-cm) rectangle.

Spread the filling out evenly on top of the dough, then sprinkle the top of the filling with the dark chocolate. Roll the dough up into a log, then slice the log into 2- to 3-inch (5- to 8-cm) rolls, and place each roll into a greased baking dish.

If making the night before, stop at this step, cover the baking dish with plastic wrap, and put it in the refrigerator. When you're ready to bake in the morning, let the dough rise on the counter, uncovered, for about 45 minutes to an hour, or until the rolls have doubled in size. Then follow the remaining baking steps. Don't let it sit longer than 14 hours.

If you're making this right away, cover the baking dish with a kitchen towel, and let the rolls rise for 30 to 45 minutes, or until doubled in size.

While the rolls rise, make the icing. In a large mixing bowl or the bowl of a stand mixer, add the cream cheese and butter, and whisk to combine. Add the vanilla, salt and about 1 cup (120 g) of the confectioners' sugar at a time until it is fully incorporated and the icing is fluffy.

Once the rolls have doubled in size, preheat the oven to 350°F (176°C). Bake the rolls for 30 to 35 minutes, or until brown on the outside and firm. Let the rolls cool for a few minutes. Spread the icing evenly on the top, and spread the cherry compote on top of that.

*See photo on page 25.

Moist 'n' Buttery Orange-Poppy Seed Bread

I was obsessed with Publix® muffins when I was a youngin'. The lemon poppy seed muffins were my favorite from their bakery, and I ate them religiously. Inspired by the nostalgia I feel every time I see them when I'm shopping, I created this fun twist on a breakfast food my father once said I ate a few too many of. Serve this melt-in-your-mouth tender bread slathered in the orange compote butter, and get ready to find your own obsession.

Serves 12

Bread
2 cups (250 g) all-purpose flour

1 tsp baking powder

1 tsp baking soda

½ tsp salt

1½ tbsp (14 g) poppy seeds

½ cup (108 g) room-temperature vegan butter

⅓ cup (67 g) organic cane sugar

1 tsp vanilla extract

2 tsp (4 g) orange zest

2 tbsp (14 g) flax meal

3 tbsp (45 ml) water

¼ cup (60 ml) applesauce

½ cup (120 ml) fresh-squeezed orange juice

½ cup (120 ml) nondairy milk

Glaze
½ cup (60 g) vegan confectioners' sugar

1 tbsp (15 ml) orange juice

1 tsp orange zest

Orange Butter
½ cup (108 g) room-temperature vegan butter

2 tsp (4 g) orange zest

Preheat the oven to 350°F (176°C). Line an 8 x 4–inch (20 x 10–cm) bread pan with parchment paper, or spray with nonstick spray.

Make the bread. In a large mixing bowl, sift together the flour, baking powder and baking soda. Stir the salt and poppy seeds into the bowl. Set aside.

In a separate large mixing bowl or the bowl of a stand mixer, add the butter and sugar, and beat together until light and fluffy, about 2 minutes. Add the vanilla and orange zest to the butter and sugar mixture, and continue to mix until fully combined, another 30 seconds or so. Set aside.

Make a flax egg. In a small mixing bowl, whisk to combine the flax meal and water. Let it sit for 3 to 5 minutes, or until it thickens. Once thickened, add the flax egg and applesauce to the butter mixture, and continue to mix until fully combined, about 1 minute. Scrape down the sides of the bowl as needed.

Begin to add the dry ingredients to the wet a little at a time, mixing together and alternating with the orange juice and the milk. Continue to alternate between wet and dry ingredients until the batter is fully combined.

Pour the batter into the prepared bread pan, smoothing the batter out evenly with a rubber spatula. Bake for 45 to 48 minutes, or until a toothpick comes out clean from the center. Let the bread cool completely.

Make the glaze. In a medium mixing bowl, whisk together the confectioners' sugar, orange juice and orange zest. Pour the glaze over the top of the bread, and smooth it out evenly with a rubber spatula. Let the glaze harden.

Meanwhile, make the butter. In a small mixing bowl, whisk together the butter and the orange zest.

When you're ready to serve, slice the bread, and either toast or serve as is with some of the orange butter.

Exceptionally
COZY MAIN MEALS

The most popular recipes on Rabbit and Wolves are almost always my comforting entrees. People consistently want and ask for cozy entrees to feed themselves and their families. I don't want to toot my own horn but, toot toot!—I happen to be pretty good at coming up with satisfying main meals that invoke a sense of comfort but are also fairly unique.

The recipes in this chapter are fun to prepare and just make people feel good, cozy and happily satiated. Be sure to try the Scratch-Made Biscuit and Broccoli Cheddar Cobbler (page 33). Savory and satisfying, you and your loved ones will gobble this up. The Fried Buffalo Chick'n Sandwiches with Blue Cheeze Dressing (page 42) are mouth-watering to prepare and incredibly rewarding to eat. I do love all things buffalo, so I could be biased. The Cheezy Hamburger Shells (page 37) are my take on a Hamburger Helper™— style meal, which of course people just feel a connection to and can't help but lick the bowl clean. Make sure to try all the recipes in this chapter. Each one has something special and flavorful for you and your favorite people to enjoy.

Scratch-Made Biscuit and Broccoli Cheddar Cobbler

This cobbler features a super creamy filling that is almost pot pie–like and is topped with cheesy black pepper biscuits that are like their own little bread dollops baked all together. You get a warm, creamy soup with a fluffy, flaky, buttery biscuit . . . all at the same time.

Serves 6

Filling

⅓ cup (72 g) vegan butter

1 small sweet onion, diced

4 cloves garlic, finely chopped

⅓ cup (41 g) all-purpose flour, plus more for dusting

3 cups (720 ml) vegetable broth

1 (16-oz [453-g]) bag frozen broccoli

2 bay leaves

2 sprigs fresh thyme

¼ tsp nutmeg

Salt and pepper, to taste

1 cup (146 g) raw cashews, soaked 8 to 12 hours

1 cup (240 ml) oat milk or other nondairy milk

2 cups (226 g) vegan Cheddar-style shreds (I prefer Violife)

Topping

2 cups (250 g) all-purpose flour

2 tsp (9 g) baking powder

1 tsp baking soda

1 tsp black pepper

1 tsp salt

½ cup (57 g) vegan Cheddar-style shreds

½ cup (108 g) cold vegan butter

½ cup (120 ml) nondairy milk

1 tsp lemon juice

Melted vegan butter or extra-virgin olive oil, for brushing

Preheat the oven to 375°F (190°C).

Make the filling. In a large pot over medium-high heat, heat the butter. Once the butter is melted, add the onion and garlic. Sauté, reducing the heat as needed, until the onion is translucent, 2 to 3 minutes. Add in the flour, and stir to combine. It should form a paste. Simmer for about 1 minute. Pour in the vegetable broth, and whisk to combine, making sure there are no lumps of flour.

Add the frozen broccoli, bay leaves, thyme, nutmeg and a pinch of salt and pepper. Bring to a simmer, reduce the heat to medium-low, and let it simmer for 10 to 15 minutes, stirring frequently.

Make the cashew cream. Drain the soaked cashews, and add them to a blender with the milk and a pinch of salt and pepper. Blend until the mixture is completely smooth.

Remove the bay leaves and thyme sprigs from the pot, and pour the cashew cream into the pot. Stir to combine. Add the Cheddar, and stir until the cheese has melted. Taste and adjust seasonings.

Pour the filling into a square 9 x 9–inch (23 x 23–cm) baking dish or a rectangular 9 x 13–inch (23 x 33–cm) baking dish. Set aside.

Make the biscuit topping. In a large mixing bowl, sift together the flour, baking powder and baking soda. Stir in the black pepper, salt and Cheddar.

Add dollops of the cold butter into the bowl, and begin to press and squeeze the butter into the dry mixture using your fingers or a fork. You want the butter to be evenly distributed and resemble sand.

In a small mixing bowl, combine the milk and lemon juice. Whisk together. Pour the milk mixture into the mixing bowl with the dry ingredients and butter. Stir to combine, and bring together into a dough ball.

Turn the dough out onto a floured surface, adding a little more flour if the dough is still sticky. Roll it out so it is about ½ inch (1.3 cm) thick, and cut large circles or squares out of the dough. You want enough to cover the filling.

Put the biscuits on top of the filling in the baking dish. Brush the tops of the biscuits with a little melted butter. Bake for 25 to 30 minutes, or until the biscuits are golden brown and cooked through. Serve immediately.

Roasted Garlic Pierogis

I know pierogies are not a quintessential kid food, but they were for me. Sometimes my mom would make them fresh, and I would get so excited to see all of the little dough circles laid out on the kitchen counter with a big bowl full of fluffy potato filling next to them. Kid-me didn't even require freshly made pierogies, as I would absolutely destroy a box of the frozen variety, too. Just know that these Roasted Garlic Pierogis trump them all.

Serves 6

Filling
1 head garlic

1 tbsp (15 ml) extra-virgin olive oil

2 large Yukon gold potatoes, peeled and diced

1 tbsp (14 g) vegan butter

⅓ cup (80 ml) vegan sour cream

½ tsp salt

½ tsp black pepper

Dough
2 cups (250 g) all-purpose flour, plus more for dusting

½ tsp salt

¼ cup (60 ml) water

½ cup (120 ml) vegan sour cream

¼ cup (54 g) room-temperature vegan butter

Toppings (Optional)
Vegan butter

Caramelized onions

Vegan sour cream

Fresh chives, chopped

Preheat the oven to 425°F (218°C).

Make the filling. Cut the top off the head of garlic, drizzle it with the olive oil and wrap the head of garlic in aluminum foil. Roast for 30 to 45 minutes, or until the head of garlic is golden brown and the cloves are very soft.

While the garlic roasts, put the potatoes in a large pot of salted water, and bring to a boil. Boil, stirring occasionally, until the potatoes are tender, 15 to 17 minutes. Drain the potatoes, then add them back to the pot. Add the butter, sour cream, salt and pepper. Mash until the mixture is smooth.

Once the garlic is done, squeeze the garlic cloves out of the skin and into the pot of mashed potatoes, stirring to incorporate. Let the potato filling cool to room temperature.

While the filling cools, make the dough. In a large mixing bowl, stir together the flour and the salt. Make a well in the center of the flour, and pour in the water, sour cream and butter.

Begin stirring the wet ingredients into the dry ingredients. Once the dough starts to come together, begin to knead the mixture with your hands until it forms a smooth ball. If the dough is still sticky, add a little more flour at a time until it is no longer sticky.

Turn the dough out onto a floured surface. Cut the dough into two pieces. Then roll each piece of dough out into a large circle that is about ⅛ inch (3 mm) thick. Using a circular biscuit cutter that is about 2 inches (5 cm) in diameter, cut circles of the dough.

Fill each circle with 1 to 2 teaspoons (5 to 10 g) of the mashed potato filling. Put the filling directly in the center, closer to one side. Wet the edges of the dough with a little bit of water. Fold the dough in half over the filling, making a half moon shape. Press down to seal. Repeat with the remaining dough.

Bring a large pot of salted water to a boil. Add the pierogies to the water, and boil for 2 to 3 minutes. The pierogies will float when they are done.

Drain and serve immediately with some butter, caramelized onions, vegan sour cream and chives, if desired.

Cheezy Hamburger Shells

This pasta dish was created in honor of the Hamburger Helper meals we all enjoyed as kids. Featuring a vegan ground beef as the star of the show, it stays true to its muse with a "meaty" flavor and texture. This savory, garlicky, creamy pasta will surely satisfy the whole family. As a one-pot meal, this recipe couldn't be easier and is the perfect dish for a busy weeknight dinner. Make extra, as it heats up well and can be enjoyed throughout the week.

Serves 6

1 tbsp (15 ml) extra-virgin olive oil

½ yellow onion, diced

4 cloves garlic, chopped

1 (12- to 16-oz [336- to 448-g]) package vegan ground beef (I prefer Beyond Beef®)

Salt and pepper, to taste

6 cups (1.4 L) vegetable broth

¼ cup (60 ml) ketchup

2 tbsp (30 ml) soy sauce or liquid aminos

16 oz (448 g) pasta shells, medium or large

½ cup (120 ml) oat milk or other nondairy milk

3 cups (339 g) vegan Cheddar-style shreds

Green onions, tomatoes and pickles, for topping (optional)

In a large nonstick skillet or pot over medium-heat, heat the olive oil. (The pot should be large enough to cook the pasta.) Add the onion and garlic, and sauté, reducing the heat as needed, for 2 to 3 minutes, until the onion is translucent.

Add the beef, breaking it up into crumbles using a wooden spoon. Toss with the onion and garlic, and sauté until the beef is brown, 8 to 10 minutes. Season with a pinch of salt and pepper. Transfer the beef, onion and garlic to a medium bowl. Set aside.

In the same skillet or pot, add the vegetable broth, ketchup, soy sauce and a pinch of salt and pepper, and whisk to combine. Heat over medium-high, and bring the liquid to a simmer. Reduce the heat to medium so it is still at a simmer but not at a high boil.

Add the pasta and stir to combine everything. Make sure the pasta is submerged in the liquid, and simmer, stirring frequently and pressing the pasta back down into the liquid until the pasta is al dente. Check your package for timing; it may need a few extra minutes. I usually simmer for about 15 minutes. The pasta will absorb most of the liquid. Reduce the heat to medium-low.

Return the beef, onion and garlic back to the skillet or pot, and toss to combine everything. Add the milk, cheese and another pinch of salt and pepper. Stir to combine everything, letting the cheese melt, and stirring a few more times until the cheese is fully melted and the sauce is creamy. Taste and adjust seasonings, adding more salt and pepper, if needed.

Serve immediately with green onions, tomatoes and/or pickles on top, if desired.

Sweet Pepper Cheezesteak Burritos

Putting together a Philly cheesesteak with a burrito is a comfort food mash-up that truly shines. A dazzling light in the darkness. A distant galaxy we can finally see with the new James Webb Telescope. The steak-seasoned soy curls, the perfect Cheez Whiz–like cheese sauce, the peppers and onions, all wrapped up with rice in a warm tortilla . . . it doesn't get better than this.

Serves 4

"Steak," Peppers and Onions

6 tbsp (90 ml) soy sauce

3 tbsp (45 ml) liquid smoke

½ cup (120 ml) extra-virgin olive oil, divided

2 tbsp (30 ml) agave syrup

1 tsp salt, plus more to taste

1 tsp smoked paprika

½ tsp black pepper, plus more to taste

½ tsp garlic powder

½ tsp onion powder

8 oz (226 g) soy curls, soaked for 10 minutes and drained

1 cup (160 g) sliced sweet onion

1 cup (150 g) sliced bell pepper, any color

4 cloves garlic, chopped

Cheeze Sauce

2 tbsp (28 g) vegan butter

2 tbsp (16 g) all-purpose flour

1½ cups (360 ml) soy milk or other nondairy milk

A few pinches of salt and pepper

1½ cups (170 g) vegan Cheddar-style cheese shreds

For Serving

4 large tortillas

1 cup (186 g) steamed white rice, divided

1 cup (112 g) vegan mozzarella-style shreds, divided

Green onions (optional)

Fresh cilantro (optional)

Vegan sour cream (optional)

Make the marinade for the soy curls. In a large mixing bowl, whisk together the soy sauce, liquid smoke, ¼ cup (60 ml) of the olive oil, the agave, salt, smoked paprika, black pepper, garlic powder and onion powder. Add the soy curls to the bowl, and toss to coat them in the marinade. Let the soy curls sit for 20 to 30 minutes.

In a large nonstick skillet over medium-high heat, heat the remaining ¼ cup (60 ml) of olive oil. Add the onion, bell pepper and garlic. Sauté, reducing the heat as needed, until the onion becomes translucent, 2 to 3 minutes. Season with a pinch of salt and pepper.

Pour the soy curls and any leftover marinade into the skillet. Sauté until the soy curls are golden brown and firm, 7 to 9 minutes. Turn off the heat.

Make the cheeze sauce. In a medium saucepan over medium heat, heat the butter. Once the butter is melted, whisk in the flour to make a roux. It will look like a paste. Let the roux simmer for 1 to 2 minutes.

Pour in the milk and a pinch of salt and pepper. Whisk to combine, making sure there are no lumps. Bring the mixture to a simmer, reduce the heat to medium-low, and let it simmer until the mixture thickens, 2 to 3 minutes. Add the Cheddar, and whisk to combine. Let the mixture simmer, whisking frequently, until the cheese melts into the sauce. Taste and adjust seasonings.

Make the burritos. Fill one tortilla with about ¼ cup (50 g) of rice, ¼ cup (28 g) of mozzarella and a quarter of the "steak," pepper and onion mixture, and drizzle with a quarter of the cheeze sauce. Top with green onions and cilantro, if desired. Fold the sides of the tortilla in, and roll into a burrito.

Serve with a little vegan sour cream and extra cheeze sauce on the side, if desired.

Legit Bangers and Mash

There is something so incredibly cozy and comforting about the idea of bangers and mash. With some bright green, buttery, salty peas on the side, my recipe is particularly special because no animals were harmed in the making of this comfy dish. But also because these bangers are simmered in beer, and some of that same beer is used for the most delicious gravy. A big bowl of these perfectly smooth mashed potatoes, with some beer-braised brats and this beer gravy, will make your evening.

Serves 4

Mash
4 lb Yukon gold potatoes, peeled and diced

4 cloves garlic

⅓ cup (72 g) vegan butter

1 cup (240 ml) nondairy milk

¼ cup (60 ml) vegan sour cream or yogurt

Salt and pepper, to taste

Bangers
12 oz (355 ml) dark vegan beer (I prefer Sierra Nevada® Stout)

4 vegan sausages (I prefer Beyond Meat brats)

Gravy
3 tbsp (42 g) vegan butter

½ sweet onion, finely chopped

4 cloves garlic, finely chopped

3 tbsp (24 g) all-purpose flour

2 cups (480 ml) vegetable broth

½ cup (120 ml) dark beer, reserved from cooking the vegan sausages

2 tbsp (30 ml) soy sauce

1 tbsp (15 ml) agave syrup

2 sprigs fresh thyme

Salt and pepper, to taste

Make the mash. In a large pot of salted water, add the potatoes and garlic, and bring to a boil. Boil until the potatoes are tender, 15 to 20 minutes.

While the potatoes boil, start the bangers. Put the beer in a large skillet. Heat over medium, and bring to a simmer. Put the sausages in the skillet with the beer. Let the sausages simmer, reducing the heat as needed, for about 10 minutes. Turn off the heat, but leave the sausages in the skillet to keep them warm.

Meanwhile, make the gravy. In a saucepan over medium heat, heat the butter. When the butter is melted, add the onion and garlic. Sauté until the onion is translucent, 2 to 3 minutes. Stir in the flour and make a paste. Simmer for another minute. Pour in the vegetable broth, then take ½ cup (120 ml) of the beer out of the skillet with the sausages, and pour that in the saucepan. Whisk to combine, making sure there are no lumps of flour.

Add the soy sauce, agave, thyme and a pinch of salt and pepper. Stir to combine. Let it simmer until the gravy is thick, 3 to 5 minutes. Remove the thyme sprigs. Reduce the heat to low, and simmer until most of the beer flavor is cooked off.

Once the potatoes are tender, drain them. Add the potatoes and garlic back to the pot, along with the butter, milk, sour cream and a few pinches of salt and pepper. Mash the potatoes and garlic with everything else until they are very smooth. Taste and adjust seasonings.

Serve a bowl of the mash with a sausage on top, covered with some gravy.

Fried Buffalo Chick'n Sandwiches with Blue Cheeze Dressing

I *adore* a good carby, flavorful sandwich. I also love buffalo sauce, so naturally I'd have to include a deliciously crispy vegan buffalo sandwich recipe in this cookbook. It also seemed appropriate to create a dreamy blue cheese dressing to slather on the bread. This sandwich is so buttery, so tangy, perfectly spicy, and the ideal sandwich for crushing those cravings. Pair with chips or French fries and blow everyone's friggin' minds.

Serves 4

Blue Cheeze Dressing

1 cup (240 ml) vegan mayonnaise

1 tbsp (15 ml) lemon juice

1 tbsp (15 ml) apple cider vinegar

1 tsp dried dill

½ tsp celery salt

1 shallot, diced

4 cloves garlic, finely chopped

3 oz (85 g) vegan blue cheese or feta crumbles

Buffalo Chick'n

1 (15-oz [425-g]) block extra-firm tofu

1 cup (240 ml) soy milk or other nondairy milk

1 tbsp (15 ml) apple cider vinegar

¾ cup (94 g) all-purpose flour

1 tsp salt

1¼ cups (70 g) panko breadcrumbs

Vegetable oil, for frying

Buffalo Sauce

12 oz (355 ml) hot sauce
(I prefer Frank's Red Hot®)

6 tbsp (84 g) vegan butter

1 tbsp (15 ml) agave syrup

Sandwiches

8 slices crusty bread

Lettuce and/or onion

Make the blue cheeze dressing. In a mixing bowl, whisk together the mayonnaise, lemon juice, apple cider vinegar, dill, celery salt, shallot and garlic. Add the cheese crumbles, and stir to combine. Put the dressing in the refrigerator until you're ready to serve the sandwiches.

Make the chick'n. Freeze the block of tofu whole to create a more porous and "meaty" texture. Thaw it in the sink. Once the tofu has thawed, cut open the package, drain it, and press the block of tofu, either with a tofu press or with a few heavy items on top of the tofu. Break the tofu into three to four large pieces.

Gather three medium mixing bowls. In the first one, add the milk and vinegar, whisk and set aside. In the second one, add the flour and salt, whisk and set aside. In the third one, add the panko breadcrumbs.

Take one piece of tofu and put it in the flour mixture, turning to coat completely. Put it in the milk mixture, turning to coat completely. Then put it back in the flour, then back in the milk. Put the tofu into the panko breadcrumbs and coat completely, patting the panko breadcrumbs onto the tofu. Repeat with all of the pieces of tofu.

In a large nonstick skillet, heat about an inch (2.5 cm) of vegetable oil. When the oil is hot, it will form tiny bubbles in the oil. Fry the tofu for 3 to 5 minutes per side, reducing the heat as needed, until the tofu is golden brown and very crispy.

Make the buffalo sauce. In a small saucepan, add the hot sauce, butter and agave. Heat over medium heat, and whisk until the butter melts. Let it simmer for 1 to 2 minutes. Turn off the heat. Either dip the tofu into the buffalo sauce, or pour the sauce over the tofu.

Make the sandwich. Take a slice of bread, spread it with the blue cheeze dressing, then put a piece of the buffalo tofu on top, followed by more blue cheeze dressing and finally lettuce and/or onion.

Toasty Muffaletta Sandwich

Meet your new go-to veganized version of a New Orleans classic! This sandwich hits all the right requirements of a mouth-watering muffaletta, and it's fun to make. The seitan is flavored and cooked to resemble salami beautifully. The layered giardiniera, vegan cheese, vegan deli meats and olive salad create that iconic rainbow of tastiness. If you're in search of an easy "sandwich night" meal with the family, this is your guy. Serve warm or cold, and don't forget to add chips. Or pair it with a pasta or potato salad for a spring or summer picnic or potluck.

Serves 6

Seitan Salami
2 tbsp (30 ml) extra-virgin olive oil
8 oz (226 g) seitan
1 tsp Dijon mustard
1 tsp agave syrup
½ tsp salt
¼ tsp black pepper
¼ tsp garlic powder
¼ tsp onion powder
1 tsp liquid smoke

Muffaletta
1 (8- to 9-inch [20- to 23-cm]) round bread loaf
1 cup (160 g) giardiniera, roughly chopped
4 oz (113 g) vegan lunch meat
2 oz (57 g) vegan provolone
2 oz (57 g) vegan mozzarella
½ cup (90 g) store-bought olive salad
2 tbsp (30 ml) extra-virgin olive oil
Pinch of salt and pepper
Pinch of dried basil
Pinch of dried oregano

Make the seitan salami. In a large nonstick skillet over medium heat, heat the olive oil. Add the seitan.

Pour the Dijon and agave into the skillet, and toss to coat the seitan. Sprinkle the salt, pepper, garlic powder, onion powder and liquid smoke over the seitan. Sauté, reducing the heat as needed, until the seitan is slightly brown, for about 5 minutes. Turn off the heat, and let it cool slightly.

While the seitan cools, prepare the rest of the sandwich. Cut off the top of the loaf of bread, and set aside. Scoop out the insides of the loaf, and reserve for another use.

Layer the sandwich. First put the giardiniera in the bottom of the loaf, and press it down. Then a layer of the lunch meat, then a layer of both the cheeses, then a layer of the seitan salami, then a layer of the olive salad.

Drizzle the inside of the top of the loaf of bread with the olive oil, and sprinkle with a pinch of salt and pepper and a pinch each of dried basil and oregano. Put the top of the loaf of bread back on top.

You can wrap the entire sandwich with plastic wrap and put it in the refrigerator. Or you can let it chill for 1 to 2 hours and serve it as a chilled sandwich. Or, preheat the oven to 350°F (176°C), bake for 20 to 25 minutes and serve the sandwich warm. Cut the sandwich into triangles to serve, no matter which temperature you serve it.

*See photo on page 43.

Caramelized Onion Barbecue Patty Melt

Man, I love a messy sandwich. This patty melt features perfect smoky barbecue lentil patties, sweet caramelized onions, French fries (yes, you read that correctly), vegan Cheddar and barbecue sauce. It's piled high and then smashed between two pieces of crusty bread. This is a pressed sandwich, the best kind of sandwich—and if you don't agree, I'm not sure this friendship can continue. This patty melt is slightly more time-consuming than your average cold-cut sandwich, but it is so very worth it.

Serves 2

Patties
2 tbsp (14 g) flax meal

3 tbsp (45 ml) water

1 cup (198 g) cooked brown lentils

¾ cup (81 g) plain vegan breadcrumbs

2 tbsp (30 ml) extra-virgin olive oil

1 tbsp (15 ml) vegan barbecue sauce

1 tsp liquid smoke

4 cloves garlic, roughly chopped

Pinch of salt and pepper

Caramelized Onions
2 tbsp (30 ml) extra-virgin olive oil

3 large sweet onions, finely sliced

2 tbsp (30 ml) agave syrup

Pinch of salt and pepper

Patty Melt
4 slices crusty vegan bread

1 cup (240 ml) barbecue sauce

2 slices vegan Cheddar cheese

½ cup (30 g) French fries, cooked

2 tbsp (30 ml) extra-virgin olive oil

Preheat the oven to 375°F (190°C). Spray a baking sheet with nonstick spray.

Make the patties. In a small bowl, whisk together the flax meal and water to make a flax egg. Set aside to thicken slightly for 1 to 2 minutes.

In a food processor, combine the lentils, flax egg, breadcrumbs, olive oil, barbecue sauce, liquid smoke, garlic and a pinch of salt and pepper. Pulse until the mixture comes together. You should be able to squeeze it together and it will stay. Form two large patties out of the lentil mixture, and place them on the prepared baking sheet. Bake for 15 minutes, flip and bake another 10 to 15 minutes, or until the patties are firm.

While the patties bake, make the caramelized onions. In a large nonstick skillet over medium-high heat, heat the olive oil. Add the onions, and sauté for about 5 minutes. Once they start to get a little brown, reduce the heat to medium-low, and continue sautéing for about 15 minutes.

When the onions are golden brown, drizzle the agave over the onions, and toss to combine. Season with a pinch of salt and pepper. Continue to sauté until the onions are a caramel color, 10 to 15 more minutes. Turn off the heat.

Once the patties are done, make the patty melts. Take 1 slice of bread, and spread about ¼ cup (60 ml) of the barbecue sauce on it. Lay a patty on top of that, then a slice of Cheddar, some of the caramelized onions, and about half of the French fries. Spread another ¼ cup (60 ml) of the barbecue sauce onto another slice of bread, and put it on top. Repeat, making another patty melt.

In a large nonstick skillet over medium heat, heat the olive oil; you can use the skillet you used to caramelize the onions. Put the patty melts into the skillet. Place something heavy on top to press them down. Let them brown for 2 to 3 minutes. Flip the patty melts, press down again and brown on that side for another 2 to 3 minutes. Make sure the cheese has melted as much as possible. Serve immediately.

*See photo on page 43.

General Tso's Tofu Wonton Soup

Two of my favorite takeout-inspired meals merge in this incredibly comforting soup. The wontons are filled with crumbled General Tso's tofu and chopped green onions, then simmered in a classic wonton soup broth. With this flavorful ground tofu filling, the world of wonton soup is now open to all.

Serves 4

Wontons
¾ cup (180 ml) vegetable broth

3 tbsp (45 ml) soy sauce

3 tbsp (42 g) vegan light brown sugar

1 tbsp (15 ml) hoisin sauce

1 tbsp (15 ml) rice wine vinegar

2 tsp (10 g) chili paste

1 tsp sesame oil

1 tsp grated ginger

1 tsp grated garlic

1 (15-oz [425-g]) block extra-firm tofu, drained and pressed

2 tbsp (30 ml) extra-virgin olive oil

3 green onions, diced

25 vegan wonton wrappers

Broth
4 cups (960 ml) vegetable broth

4 cloves garlic, grated

1 (½-inch [1.3-cm]) piece fresh ginger, grated

3 tbsp (45 ml) soy sauce, plus more as needed

2 tbsp (26 g) organic cane sugar

1 tbsp (15 ml) rice wine vinegar, plus more as needed

½ tsp sesame oil

1 shallot, sliced

2 green onions, roughly chopped

Baby bok choy or other vegetables, for serving

Make the wontons. In a large mixing bowl, whisk together the vegetable broth, soy sauce, brown sugar, hoisin sauce, rice wine vinegar, chili paste, sesame oil, ginger and garlic.

Crumble the tofu into very small crumbles. Add it to the bowl with the marinade. Toss to coat all of the tofu, and make sure the tofu is as submerged in the marinade as possible. Marinate the tofu for at least 4 hours and up to overnight.

When you are ready to make the soup, in a large nonstick skillet over medium-high heat, heat the olive oil. Pour the tofu into the skillet, marinade and all. Sauté, reducing the heat as needed, for 15 to 18 minutes, or until the marinade has thickened and absorbed and the tofu is starting to brown.

Put the tofu into a mixing bowl, and add the green onions. Toss to combine. Let the tofu cool to room temperature.

Take a wonton wrapper, and dab the edges of the wrapper with water using your finger. Fill the center of each wrapper with about 1 to 2 teaspoons (5 to 10 g) of the tofu filling. Fold in half along the diagonal to create a triangle and press the edges of the wrapper together. Repeat with all of the wontons. Set aside.

Make the broth. Pour the vegetable broth into a large pot and heat over medium-high. Once it comes to a simmer, reduce the heat to medium-low, and add the garlic, ginger, soy sauce, cane sugar, rice wine vinegar, sesame oil, shallot and green onions. Stir to combine. Let the broth simmer for 15 to 17 minutes. Taste and adjust seasonings, adding more soy sauce or rice wine vinegar, if needed.

While the broth simmers, bring a separate large pot of water to a boil, and boil the wontons for 3 to 4 minutes. They are done when they float. Drain the wontons.

Once the broth has simmered, divide the broth evenly among four bowls. Add the wontons to each bowl, and top with bok choy or any vegetables you like, stirring them into the broth so they steam. Serve immediately.

Creamy "Sausage" and Gnocchi Soup

I dare you to think of a more comforting combo than cream, sausage and gnocchi. I'll wait.

With pillowy potato dumplings, the meaty vegan sausage and the creamy, cheesy broth, this soup just hits different. I have always loved gnocchi in a cream sauce, and since going vegan, I have loved experimenting with dairy-free cream sauces for my gnocchi. Turning that combo into a soup is the best idea I've ever had. Herbs, white wine and tomatoes ramp up this recipe even more. You'll find yourself stockpiling gnocchi just so you can make this soup.

Serves 6

1 cup (146 g) raw cashews

1 cup (240 ml) almond milk or other nondairy milk

Salt and pepper, to taste

4 vegan sausages, sliced

1 lb (454 g) grape tomatoes

3 tbsp (45 ml) extra-virgin olive oil, divided

4 cloves garlic, finely chopped

½ sweet onion, diced

½ tsp dried oregano

½ tsp dried basil

¼ cup (60 ml) vegan white wine

6 cups (1.4 L) vegetable broth

1 lb (454 g) vegan gnocchi

⅓ cup (33 g) vegan Parmesan

1 tsp lemon juice

Fresh basil, for serving (optional)

Preheat the oven to 425°F (218°C).

Soak the cashews for 6 to 8 hours in room-temperature water, or boil them for 15 to 20 minutes. They should be soft and light in color. Drain once they are ready.

In a blender, combine the drained cashews with the milk and a pinch of salt and pepper. Blend on high until the mixture is very smooth. Set aside.

Put the sausages and the grape tomatoes on a baking sheet, and drizzle them with 1 tablespoon of the olive oil and a pinch of salt and pepper. Toss to coat. Roast in the oven for 15 minutes, toss them and roast for another 10 to 15 minutes, or until the sausages are brown and the tomatoes have burst.

While the sausages and tomatoes roast, start the soup. In a large soup pot over medium heat, heat the remaining 2 tablespoons (30 ml) of olive oil. Add the garlic and onion, and sauté, reducing the heat as needed, for 3 to 4 minutes, or until the onion is translucent. Sprinkle the oregano, basil and a pinch of salt and pepper over the garlic and onion, and stir to combine.

Pour the wine into the pot, and simmer for 2 to 3 minutes, or until the wine has absorbed into the garlic and onion. Pour the vegetable broth into the pot, as well as a few pinches of salt and pepper. Stir and bring to a simmer. Reduce the heat to medium-low. Add the gnocchi, and simmer for as long as the package directions recommend.

Pour the cashew cream sauce into the pot, and whisk to combine. Add the Parmesan and lemon juice, and whisk to combine again.

Once the sausage and tomatoes are done, add them to the pot as well. Stir to combine. Taste and adjust seasonings. You may need more salt and pepper.

Serve immediately with fresh basil, if desired.

*See photo on page 46.

Peppery Chili Frito Pie

This recipe is perfect for when you need a low-effort, one-pot meal. Maybe you're feeling under the weather, or maybe it's just really cold outside and you want to cozy up with a warm, yummy meal. Either way, it's a comforting dish.

This is also a great get-together meal. Having an autumn bonfire party? Have snack packs of your favorite corn chips handy, and pour this spicy chili on top for a fun mobile meal.

Serves 4

1 tbsp (15 ml) extra-virgin olive oil

½ white onion, diced

4 cloves garlic, finely chopped

2 tbsp (32 g) tomato paste

1 (15.5-oz [439-g]) can black beans, drained and rinsed

1 (15.5-oz [439-g]) can kidney beans, drained and rinsed

1 tbsp (8 g) chili powder

1 tsp cumin

1 tsp dried oregano

Pinch of cayenne

1 (28-oz [794-g]) can crushed tomatoes

1 (4-oz [113-g]) can green chilies

Salt and pepper, to taste

1 (9.25-oz [262-g]) bag Fritos® or corn chips

Sliced jalapeños

Vegan Cheddar cheese

Vegan sour cream

In a large pot over medium heat, heat the olive oil. Add the onion and garlic and sauté, reducing the heat as needed, for 2 to 3 minutes, or until the onion is translucent. Add the tomato paste, and stir it into the onion and garlic.

Add the black beans, kidney beans, chili powder, cumin, oregano and cayenne. Stir to combine. Bring to a simmer, then add the crushed tomatoes, green chilies and a pinch of salt and pepper. Stir to combine. Bring to a simmer, reduce the heat to medium-low, and allow to cook, stirring occasionally, for 15 to 20 minutes, or until the mixture is nice and thick. Taste and adjust seasonings. Turn off the heat.

Put about a quarter of the Fritos into a bowl, and top them with some of the chili, jalapeños, cheese and sour cream. Serve immediately.

*See photo on page 51.

Crispy Cheezeburger Tacos

A "cheese" burger in a taco?! Yes, it's true. Get your burger fix in the form of a crispy taco. You can feed the whole family with this easy and oh-so-cozy recipe. Just brown the vegan beef, throw in some extras and sauté. Then fill your tacos and bake for an easy 30-minute meal.

When you're ready to eat, dip the perfectly crispy taco in the tangy burger sauce, take a bite, and make your taste buds incredibly happy.

Serves 8

Burger Sauce
½ cup (120 ml) vegan mayonnaise

1 tbsp (15 ml) ketchup

1 tbsp (15 g) sweet relish

1 tsp Dijon mustard

Pinch of black pepper

Pinch of paprika

Crispy Cheezeburger Tacos
1 tbsp (15 ml) extra-virgin olive oil

12 oz (340 g) vegan ground beef

1 tbsp (16 g) tomato paste

1 tbsp (15 ml) Dijon mustard

⅓ cup (80 ml) vegetable broth

8 oz (226 g) vegan Cheddar-style cheese shreds, divided

8 flour or corn tortillas

Diced onion

Diced pickles

Shredded lettuce

Diced tomatoes

Oil, for brushing the tortillas

Make the burger sauce. In a small mixing bowl, add the mayonnaise, ketchup, sweet relish, Dijon and a pinch of pepper and paprika, and whisk to combine. Put the bowl of sauce in the refrigerator until ready to serve.

Preheat the oven to 425° (218°C).

Make the filling. In a large nonstick skillet over medium-high heat, heat the olive oil. Add the ground beef, and break it up with a wooden spoon. Sauté, reducing the heat as needed, until the beef has browned, 3 to 5 minutes. Add the tomato paste, Dijon and vegetable broth, and stir to combine everything. Sauté for 1 to 2 minutes.

Add 4 ounces (113 g) of the Cheddar shreds to the skillet, reserving the rest for topping the tacos. Stir the cheese into the beef, and let it melt.

Once the cheese has melted, turn off the heat. Take your tortillas, and add about ¼ cup (57 g) of the beef to one side of the tortilla, spreading it out.

Top the taco with some of the remaining cheddar shreds, onion, pickles, lettuce and tomatoes. Fold the empty side of the tortilla over the other side, and press down. Repeat with all the beef.

Brush both sides of each taco with oil, and place them on a baking sheet. Bake for 10 to 15 minutes, or until the tacos are golden brown and crispy.

Serve with the burger sauce for dipping.

Lauren's Favorite Pizza

Let me explain why this is my very favorite pizza. First, I crave sweet and spicy foods. So these candied jalapeños are a dream come true. The combination of barbecue soy curls that mimic chicken in the best way and the creamy vegan ranch is awe-inspiring. All these yummy toppings with some vegan mozzarella and extra vegan ranch for dipping will have you swooning. You can even make the candied jalapeños a day ahead and let them sit in the refrigerator until you are ready to make the pizza. I'm going to go out on a limb here and say this is about to be *our* favorite pizza.

Serves 8

Candied Jalapeños
¼ cup (60 ml) apple cider vinegar

⅓ cup (67 g) organic cane sugar

3 cloves garlic, smashed

2 jalapeños, thinly sliced

Barbecue Soy Curls
2 tbsp (30 ml) extra-virgin olive oil

4 oz (113 g) soy curls, soaked and drained

½ cup (120 ml) vegan barbecue sauce

Pizza
1 lb (454 g) vegan pizza dough (I prefer Trader Joe's)

Flour, for dusting

½ cup (120 ml) vegan barbecue sauce

1½ cups (170 g) vegan mozzarella (I prefer Miyoko's)

½ cup (120 ml) vegan ranch, plus more for serving (I prefer Hidden Valley®)

Fresh chives, for topping

Make the candied jalapeños. In a small saucepan, whisk together the apple cider vinegar, sugar and garlic. Heat the saucepan over medium heat. Bring to a simmer, then reduce the heat to low. Let the mixture simmer until the sugar is fully dissolved, 1 to 2 minutes.

Put the jalapeños in a heat-proof bowl. Pour the hot vinegar mixture over the jalapeños. Press the jalapeños down into the mixture with a spoon. Let the jalapeños sit on the counter until cool. Then let the jalapeños cool completely in the refrigerator. You want to let them sit in the liquid for at least 2 hours.

When you are ready to make the pizza, preheat the oven to 450°F (232°C). Spray a pizza pan with nonstick spray.

Cook the soy curls. In a large nonstick skillet over medium-high heat, heat the olive oil. Add the soy curls and sauté, reducing the heat as needed, until they are golden brown and crispy, 8 to 10 minutes. Pour in the barbecue sauce, and toss to coat. Sauté for another 1 to 2 minutes. Remove from the heat.

Make the pizza. Roll the pizza dough out on a floured surface into a large circle, whatever thickness you like your pizza crust. Place on the prepared pizza pan.

Spread the barbecue sauce for the pizza out evenly onto the dough, leaving an edge for the crust. Spread the mozzarella evenly on top of the barbecue sauce. Sprinkle the barbecue soy curls and candied jalapeños out over the mozzarella. Bake for 12 to 15 minutes, or until the pizza is cooked through and the bottom of the crust is golden brown.

Once the pizza is done, drizzle with ½ cup (120 ml) of the ranch and sprinkle with chives. Cut into slices, and serve with extra ranch, if desired.

*See photo on page 30.

Spicy Lemon-Butter Tofu and Cheezy Polenta

We all have those days when carb y, savory, cheesy goodness is all you can think about. There is no better way to satisfy that craving than with this recipe. The tofu is generously coated in Cajun seasoning and baked until golden brown, then served on top of the most luscious polenta. Just when you thought this meal couldn't possibly get any better, you drizzle a lemon-butter sauce on top of it all. This is it: the perfect bowl of delicious comfort.

Serves 4

Spicy Tofu
1 (15-oz [425-g]) block extra-firm tofu, drained and pressed, cut into cubes

2 tbsp (30 ml) extra-virgin olive oil

2 tsp (10 g) Cajun seasoning

1 tsp salt

Cheezy Polenta
6 tbsp (84 g) vegan butter, divided

3 cups (720 ml) soy milk or other nondairy milk

1 cup (125 g) polenta

½ cup (57 g) vegan Cheddar-style shreds

Salt and pepper, to taste

1 tbsp (3 g) fresh chives, plus more for serving (optional)

Lemon-Butter Sauce
¼ cup (54 g) vegan butter

10 cloves garlic, finely chopped

½ tsp lemon zest

1 tbsp (15 ml) lemon juice

1 tsp Cajun seasoning

2 sprigs fresh thyme

Salt and pepper, to taste

Preheat the oven to 400°F (204°C). Line a baking sheet with parchment paper or spray with nonstick spray.

Make the tofu. In a large mixing bowl, add the tofu, drizzle with the olive oil and sprinkle the Cajun seasoning and salt on top. Toss the tofu with a rubber spatula to combine everything.

Spread the tofu out in a single layer on the prepared baking sheet. Bake for 15 minutes, flip the tofu with a fork or spatula, and bake for another 15 minutes, or until firm and golden brown.

While the tofu bakes, make the cheezy polenta. In a medium saucepan over medium-high heat, heat 4 tablespoons (54 g) of the butter and the milk. The butter will melt. Bring to a simmer, then reduce the heat to medium-low.

Very slowly, add the polenta to the simmering liquid, just a little at a time so the polenta doesn't clump together. Whisk constantly until the polenta is completely incorporated. Reduce the heat to low, cover the saucepan, and let the polenta simmer for 5 to 10 minutes. You can check the polenta package for exact timing. Once the polenta has absorbed all the liquid and is soft, turn off the heat.

Add the remaining 2 tablespoons (28 g) of butter, the cheese and a few pinches of salt and pepper. Whisk to combine, letting the butter and cheese melt into the polenta. Taste and adjust seasonings. Stir in some chives, if desired.

Once the polenta is done, leave it on the stove with the lid on to keep warm.

Make the lemon-butter sauce. In a medium nonstick skillet over medium heat, heat the butter. Let the butter melt, then add the garlic, lemon zest, lemon juice, Cajun seasoning, thyme and a pinch of salt and pepper. Reduce the heat to low, and simmer for 1 to 2 minutes. Remove and discard the thyme sprigs. Remove the sauce from the heat.

Once the tofu is done, serve a bowl of the cheezy polenta with the tofu on top, drizzled with the lemon-butter sauce. Top with chives, if desired.

*See photo on page 54.

Crispy Mango Tofu with Fried Rice

The flavor of this tofu has everything! It is sweet, salty, tangy and a little spicy. The only thing I can think of that makes it better is serving it over some perfectly fried rice. So much more access to vegan products makes everything super easy now. I have missed fried rice with egg in it for years. This vegetable and "egg" fried rice makes me do a little kitchen dance.

Serves 4

Mango Tofu

1 (15-oz [425-g]) block extra-firm tofu, drained and pressed, cut into cubes

6 tbsp (90 ml) extra-virgin olive oil, divided

⅓ cup (43 g) cornstarch

Pinch of salt and pepper

2 tbsp (30 ml) ketchup

2 tbsp (30 ml) chili sauce

2 tbsp (30 ml) soy sauce

2 tbsp (30 ml) agave syrup

2 tbsp (30 ml) mango juice

1 tsp rice wine vinegar

1 cup (150 g) chopped red bell pepper

1 cup (165 g) chopped mango

1 (1-inch [2.5-cm]) piece fresh ginger, grated

Fried Rice

2 tbsp (30 ml) extra-virgin olive oil

½ sweet onion, diced

1 large carrot, diced

4 cloves garlic, finely chopped

½ cup (67 g) frozen peas

3 oz (85 g) baby corn (canned or fresh)

⅓ cup (80 ml) vegan egg

1 cup (186 g) cooked white rice

2 tbsp (30 ml) soy sauce

2 tbsp (30 ml) sesame oil

2 tbsp (30 ml) rice wine vinegar

2 green onions, chopped, plus more for serving

Preheat the oven to 400°F (204°C). Line a large baking sheet with parchment paper or a silicone mat.

Make the tofu. In a medium mixing bowl, combine the tofu with 2 tablespoons (30 ml) of the olive oil, tossing to coat. Sprinkle the cornstarch and a pinch of salt and pepper over the tofu. Toss to coat. Lay the tofu in a single layer on the prepared baking sheet. Bake for 15 minutes, flip the tofu, and bake for another 15 to 20 minutes, or until the tofu is firm and crispy on the outside.

In a medium mixing bowl, whisk together 2 tablespoons (30 ml) of the olive oil, the ketchup, chili sauce, soy sauce, agave, mango juice and vinegar. Set aside.

Make the fried rice. In a large nonstick skillet or wok over medium heat, heat the olive oil. Add the onion, carrot, garlic, peas and baby corn. Sauté for 2 to 3 minutes, or until the onion is translucent. Add the egg, and stir together with the veggies to "scramble" the egg. Let it cook for about 2 minutes.

Add the rice, soy sauce, sesame oil, vinegar and green onions. Toss to combine everything. Let the rice fry for 5 to 6 minutes, or until it is brown and you have some crispy edges. Taste and adjust seasonings. Reduce the heat to low to keep warm while you finish the tofu.

Once the tofu is done baking, in a large nonstick skillet over medium-high heat, heat the remaining 2 tablespoons (30 ml) of olive oil for the tofu. Add the bell pepper, mango and ginger, and sauté for 2 to 3 minutes. Pour the sauce into the skillet. Bring to a simmer, reduce the heat to medium-low, and let the sauce simmer for 4 to 5 minutes, or until it has thickened slightly. Add the baked tofu to the skillet, and toss in the sauce.

Serve immediately. Put some of the fried rice in a bowl, and top with some of the tofu and more green onions on top, if desired.

Scrumptious
ONE-POT WEEKNIGHT DINNERS

As a parent, I recognize how important it is to have go-to recipes during the week that are easy and fast. Weeknights are filled with soccer practice, homework, staying late at work, running errands or being stuck in traffic. And that's only a few instances!

Maybe you're looking for a dish to make for a dear friend who's sick with the flu. A big bowl of the Simple Lemongrass Noodle Soup (page 74) will warm them right up. Your neighbors just had a baby, and you'd like to make them something easy in between your weekly meal rotation? The Creamy Toscana Rigatoni (page 70) is a simple dish that can be reheated as needed and will make them feel loved and cared for with each bite. No matter the occasion, I've got you covered in this chapter.

Easy is the name of the game here. One-pot or one-pan meals are the epitome of simple. Why? Because you can throw everything into one pan, cook it, then serve it or pack it up. Not too many steps go into these recipes, and you'll love how delicious they are to boot. From the Beer-Braised Black Bean Chili (page 60) to Terry's Tikka Masala–Inspired Tofu (page 76), in this chapter you'll find flavorful and ridiculously easy recipes that you'll be proud to share with your family or friends.

One-Skillet Chipotle Tortilla Rice Bake

This rice bake is like deep-dish nachos, and you are worthy of experiencing deep-dish nachos. With rice, black beans, tortilla chips and vegan cheese melted on top, this is the fusion you're looking for when you can't decide between nachos and a hearty burrito. Since turning 37, all I can muster up for dinner sometimes is something that can be made in just one pot. It satisfies all cravings; you know, the ones where you just want to sit with your feet up, under some blankets, eating cheese, chips, rice and sauces.

Serves 6

2 tbsp (30 ml) extra-virgin olive oil

½ red onion, diced

6 cloves garlic, finely chopped

1 (15.5-oz [439-g]) can black beans, drained and rinsed

1 chipotle pepper in adobo sauce, chopped

1 tsp adobo sauce from the can of chipotles

1 tsp smoked paprika

1 tsp cumin

1 tsp salt

1 tsp lime juice

1 (28-oz [794-g]) can crushed tomatoes

2 cups (480 ml) water

1½ cups (300 g) long-grain rice

1½ cups (170 g) vegan Cheddar-style shreds

2 cups (52 g) tortilla chips

Preheat the oven to 425°F (218°C).

In a large, oven-safe, nonstick skillet over medium-high heat, heat the olive oil. Add the red onion and garlic to the skillet. Sauté, reducing the heat as needed, until the onion is translucent, 1 to 2 minutes.

Pour the black beans, chipotle pepper, adobo sauce, smoked paprika, cumin, salt and lime juice into the skillet. Stir to combine everything, and simmer for about 1 minute. Add the crushed tomatoes and water to the skillet, and stir to combine. Bring to a simmer, reduce the heat to medium-low, and keep at a simmer.

Pour the rice into the skillet and simmer, stirring occasionally, for 15 to 17 minutes, or until the rice has softened and most of the liquid has been absorbed. Smooth the rice out on top with a rubber spatula.

Spread half the cheese over the top of the rice. Press the tortilla chips on top of the cheese, pressing them down in the rice slightly and covering the entire top of the skillet. Sprinkle the remaining cheese over the top of the tortilla chips. Transfer the skillet to the oven, and bake for 10 minutes. The cheese should melt, and the tortilla chips should brown slightly.

Serve a scoop of the tortilla rice bake in a bowl with any toppings you would normally serve on a taco.

Beer-Braised Black Bean Chili

As I've gotten older, my appreciation for a good chili has become more vast each time I eat it. This chili, with beer, black beans and amazing spice, is a true charmer. This is made all in one pot and is great on days when you don't really feel like cooking but you know you probably should. Hearty, a little spicy and with such depth of flavor (hello, maple syrup!), it really is a dish that you can just sit down and enjoy. Top with all the good stuff: chips, salsa, cilantro, black olives or vegan sour cream.

Serves 4

2 tbsp (30 ml) extra-virgin olive oil

½ red onion, diced

3 sweet peppers or 2 bell peppers, diced

1 jalapeño, deseeded and diced

4 cloves garlic, finely chopped

2 tbsp (32 g) tomato paste

12 oz (355 ml) beer (I prefer a stout)

1 (15.5-oz [439-g]) can kidney beans, drained and rinsed

2 (15.5-oz [439-g]) cans black beans, drained and rinsed

1 tbsp (8 g) chili powder

1 tsp cumin

1 tsp dried oregano

1 tsp salt

½ tsp smoked paprika

Pinch of red pepper flakes

Pinch of ground cinnamon

1 (28-oz [794-g]) can crushed tomatoes

2 tbsp (30 ml) maple syrup

Toppings (Optional)
Tortilla chips

Salsa

Fresh cilantro

Fresh chives

Black olives

Peppers

In a large pot over medium-high heat, heat the olive oil. Add the red onion, peppers, jalapeño and garlic to the pot. Sauté, reducing the heat as needed, until the onion is translucent, 1 to 2 minutes. Add the tomato paste, stir to combine with the veggies and sauté for another minute.

Pour the beer into the pot, and stir to combine. Bring to a simmer, and reduce the heat to medium-low.

In a small bowl, add the kidney beans, and mash them with a potato masher or fork until most of them are mashed and resemble refried beans.

To the pot, add the black beans, mashed kidney beans, chili powder, cumin, dried oregano, salt, smoked paprika, red pepper flakes and cinnamon. Stir to combine everything, and simmer for 10 to 12 minutes.

Pour the crushed tomatoes and maple syrup into the pot, stir to combine and continue simmering, stirring frequently, for 10 to 15 more minutes. Taste and adjust seasonings.

Serve the chili in a bowl topped with tortilla chips, salsa, cilantro, chives, black olives and/or peppers, if desired. The chili keeps in the refrigerator for about a week and reheats very well.

*See photo on page 58.

Spicy Lasagna Soup

If you haven't tried my white lasagna soup yet—the soup that broke the Internet—here's your chance to try an upgraded version. In honor of one of my most-loved recipes, I made this super cozy, creamy, decadent soup. I added some spicy vegan sausage, which frankly makes everything better. Plus, to simply give the appearance of a healthy food, I added some fresh spinach. This lush, swanky soup will be on repeat all fall and winter, and no one will be mad about it.

Serves 4

1 cup (146 g) raw cashews

1 cup (240 ml) soy milk or other nondairy milk

Salt and pepper, to taste

2 tbsp (30 ml) extra-virgin olive oil

6 cloves garlic, finely chopped

½ sweet onion, diced

4 spicy vegan sausages, casings removed

1 pint (298 g) grape tomatoes

1 tbsp (14 g) tomato paste

1 tsp dried oregano

1 tsp dried basil

6 cups (1.4 L) vegetable broth

¼ cup (20 g) nutritional yeast

2 tsp (10 ml) agave syrup

1 tsp lemon juice

8 lasagna sheets

2 cups (60 g) spinach

A few pinches of red pepper flakes

Vegan Parmesan, for serving (optional)

Chopped fresh herbs, for serving (optional)

Soak the cashews in room-temperature water for 8 hours or overnight, or boil them for 15 to 20 minutes.

Make the cashew cream. Drain the soaked cashews, and add them to a blender with the milk and a pinch of salt and pepper. Blend on high, scraping down the sides as needed, until the cashew cream is very smooth. Set aside.

In a large soup pot over medium-high heat, heat the olive oil. Add the garlic and onion. Crumble the sausage into the pot. Sauté, reducing the heat as needed, until the sausage is brown, 2 to 3 minutes. Add the grape tomatoes and a pinch of salt and pepper, and continue to sauté until the grape tomatoes burst open. Transfer everything—the garlic, onions, sausages and tomatoes—from the pot into a large bowl, and set aside.

Add the tomato paste, dried oregano and dried basil to the pot, and sauté for 1 minute. Pour in the vegetable broth, cashew cream, nutritional yeast, agave, lemon juice and a pinch of salt and pepper. Whisk to combine. Bring to a simmer, reduce the heat to medium and have the liquid at a small bubble.

Break the lasagna sheets up into 1- to 2-inch (2.5- to 5-cm) pieces. Add them to the pot, and simmer until they are al dente, 15 to 20 minutes. Check your package for timing. Add the spinach, stir and let it wilt in the soup for just a minute.

Add in a few pinches of red pepper flakes to the pot. Return the garlic, onion, sausages and tomatoes to the pot. Stir to combine everything. Taste and adjust seasonings, adding more salt and pepper if needed.

Serve immediately, with Parmesan and herbs on top, if desired.

*See photo on page 63.

Tinga Taco Soup with Rice

You can probably tell, since I dedicated an entire chapter to them, that I love one-pot meals—and it doesn't get much easier than this one. With a lovely smoky chipotle flavor, this soup is incredibly filling. It's perfect for a cool night, when you want something cozy but don't feel like cooking. It features Mexican oregano, which has a citrus undertone rather than its minty Italian cousin. This soup can be topped with all your favorite taco accoutrements: vegan cheese, cilantro, green onions, olives and rice. I thoroughly enjoy setting this soup up buffet-style with all kinds of toppings and letting people make their own bowls.

Serves 4

1 tbsp (15 ml) extra-virgin olive oil

½ sweet onion, diced

4 cloves garlic, finely chopped

2 chipotles, diced

1 tbsp (15 ml) adobo sauce, from the can of chipotles

2 (15.5-oz [439-g]) cans black beans, drained and rinsed

1 (15.5-oz [439-g]) can pinto beans, drained and rinsed

½ tsp Mexican oregano

1 tsp cumin

½ tsp chili powder

Salt and pepper, to taste

2 cups (480 ml) vegetable broth

1 (15-oz [425-g]) can tomato sauce

1 tsp lime juice, plus more as needed

Vegan Cheddar-style shreds, fresh cilantro and steamed white rice, for serving (optional)

In a large soup pot over medium-high heat, heat the olive oil. Add the onion and garlic. Sauté, reducing the heat, until the onion is translucent, 2 to 3 minutes. Add the chipotle and adobo sauce, and sauté for another minute.

Pour in the black beans, pinto beans, Mexican oregano, cumin, chili powder and a pinch of salt and pepper. Stir to combine.

Add the vegetable broth, tomato sauce, lime juice and another pinch of salt and pepper. Stir to combine everything. Bring to a simmer, reduce the heat to medium-low, and let it simmer, stirring frequently, for 15 to 20 minutes. Taste and adjust seasonings, adding more salt, pepper or lime, if needed.

Serve with Cheddar cheese, cilantro and/or rice, if desired.

Cheezy Spinach and Artichoke Dip Pasta Bake

I hate to admit it, but in my late teens and early twenties I frequented TGI Friday's™. The spinach and artichoke dip was my freaking jam. Cut to my late thirties, and I still crave that stuff. This fancier, pasta-fied version hits the spot. It is creamy and cheesy; the classic combination of spinach and artichoke is just the tops. The pasta gives you all the carbs you need to replace the chips. If you are a spinach and artichoke dip lover like I am, this will please you to no end.

Serves 4

2 tbsp (30 ml) extra-virgin olive oil

8 cloves garlic, finely chopped

1 (14-oz [397-g]) can artichoke hearts, roughly chopped

1 (1-lb [453-g]) bag frozen spinach, thawed and drained

Salt and pepper, to taste

4 oz (113 g) vegan cream cheese

¼ cup (54 g) vegan butter

¼ cup (31 g) all-purpose flour

3 cups (720 ml) vegetable broth

1½ cups (360 ml) almond milk or other nondairy milk

12 oz (340 g) rigatoni or other short pasta

¼ cup (25 g) vegan Parmesan, plus more for serving

½ cup (28 g) panko breadcrumbs or crushed potato chips

½ cup (56 g) vegan mozzarella

Red pepper flakes (optional)

Preheat the oven to 450°F (232°C).

In a large oven-safe pot over medium-high heat, heat the olive oil. Add the garlic, artichoke hearts and spinach. Season with a pinch of salt and pepper. Sauté, reducing the heat as needed, for about 5 minutes.

Stir in the cream cheese, letting it melt into the spinach mixture. Stir until everything is fully combined. Transfer the spinach mixture to a bowl, and set aside. Reduce the heat to medium.

To the same pot, add the butter. Let the butter melt, then pour in the flour. Whisk the flour into the butter until it is fully combined. This will form a roux. Let the roux simmer for 1 to 2 minutes.

Pour the vegetable broth and milk into the pot. Whisk to combine the liquid with the roux, making sure there are no lumps. Season with a few pinches of salt and pepper, and bring to a simmer.

Once the liquid is simmering, add the pasta, and stir to combine. Make sure the pasta is submerged in the liquid. Let the pasta simmer for 7 to 9 minutes, stirring frequently. The pasta should still be a bit firm, but most of the liquid should be thick and absorbed.

Add the spinach and artichoke mixture back into the pot, and stir to combine everything. Taste and adjust seasonings. It may need more salt and pepper.

Spread the pasta out evenly in the pot with a rubber spatula, then top with the Parmesan. Top that with the panko breadcrumbs and the mozzarella. Bake in the pot, uncovered, for 10 to 11 minutes. The cheese should melt as much as possible and the top should brown.

Serve with extra Parmesan and red pepper flakes, if desired.

Caramelized "Honey"-Garlic Veggie Pitas

You may be thinking, how comforting could a pita filled with vegetables possibly be? However, I need you to understand that these vegetables are roasted until they are juicy and golden brown and covered in a sweet, tangy and salty sauce that is nothing short of a nectar of the gods. Then they are stuffed into a warm pita pocket that has first been filled with hummus, and they're topped off with lettuce, red onion and vegan feta. I assure you, these pitas will have you rethinking the idea of vegetables being comfort food.

Serves 4

8 cloves garlic, finely chopped

⅓ cup (80 ml) light agave syrup

¼ cup (60 ml) vegetable broth

2 tbsp (30 ml) white wine vinegar

1 tbsp (15 ml) liquid aminos or soy sauce

6 cups vegetables, roughly chopped (such as mushrooms, peppers, green beans, Brussels sprouts and broccoli)

1 tbsp (15 ml) extra-virgin olive oil

Pinch of salt and pepper

4 pitas

⅓ cup (83 g) hummus

Lettuce, red onion and vegan feta, for topping

Preheat the oven to 375°F (190°C).

Make the "honey"-garlic sauce. In a medium mixing bowl, add the garlic. Pour in the agave, vegetable broth, white wine vinegar and liquid aminos. Whisk to combine. Set aside.

Make the vegetables. In a large mixing bowl, add all of the vegetables, and drizzle the oil over top. Sprinkle a pinch of salt and pepper, and toss with a rubber spatula to coat the vegetables.

Pour half the "honey"-garlic sauce over the vegetables, and toss to coat them. Reserve the other half for later.

Pour the vegetables and any excess sauce that is in the bowl onto a large baking sheet. Spread them out with the rubber spatula into a single layer. Roast the vegetables for 15 minutes.

Remove the vegetables from the oven, pour the remaining sauce over the vegetables, toss, and spread back out on the baking sheet. Roast for 15 more minutes, or until the vegetables are tender and have browned a bit. Most of the sauce should be absorbed and thickened slightly.

Warm your pitas in the oven for 2 to 3 minutes, if desired. Cut them in half. Spread 1 to 2 tablespoons (14 to 28 g) of hummus on the inside of each pita pocket. Fill with the roasted vegetables. Top with lettuce, red onion and feta, if desired. Serve immediately.

Loaded Baked Potato Soup

Calling all potato lovers! This hearty soup is inspired by your classic loaded baked potato. This perfect cozy weeknight meal features sautéed mushrooms that mimic bacon in flavor. It's a one-pot beauty, so when you're midway through the week and just want to throw things in a pan, this recipe will be your new BFF. Creamy and buttery, you'll enjoy all the flavors of a savory baked potato in soup form. Honestly, what more can you ask for?

Serves 6

1½ cups (219 g) raw cashews

4 large russet potatoes

1½ cups (360 ml) almond milk or other nondairy milk

Salt and pepper, to taste

1 tbsp (15 ml) extra-virgin olive oil

5 oz (142 g) shiitake mushrooms, thinly sliced

1 tbsp (15 ml) liquid smoke

2 tbsp (30 ml) soy sauce or liquid aminos

2 tbsp (30 ml) maple syrup

½ tsp smoked paprika

2 tbsp (28 g) vegan butter

⅓ cup (53 g) sweet onion, diced

6 cloves garlic, finely chopped

4 cups (960 ml) vegetable broth

1 cup (113 g) vegan Cheddar-style shreds, plus more for topping

½ tsp garlic powder

Fresh chives or green onions, for topping (optional)

Soak the cashews in room-temperature water for 8 to 12 hours, or boil them for 15 to 20 minutes.

Pierce the outside of each potato a few times with a fork. Microwave the potatoes for 10 to 12 minutes. They should be tender but not completely cooked through. Let the potatoes cool for a few minutes, then cut them into small chunks.

Make the cashew cream. Drain the soaked cashews, and add them to a blender with the milk and a pinch of salt and pepper. Blend on high until the cashew cream is completely smooth, and set aside.

In a large soup pot over medium-high heat, heat the olive oil. Add the mushrooms and sauté, reducing the heat as needed, for 1 to 2 minutes. Pour the liquid smoke, soy sauce, maple syrup and smoked paprika over the mushrooms. Toss to coat, and reduce the heat to medium-low. Continue to sauté the mushrooms until they have browned a little and all the liquid has been absorbed, 5 to 7 minutes.

Remove the mushrooms and any excess sauce from the pot, and set aside in a small bowl. The mushrooms will be one of your toppings.

In the same pot over medium-high heat, add the butter. Once the butter is melted, add the onion and garlic. Sauté, reducing the heat as needed, until the onion is translucent, about 2 minutes. Add the potatoes and toss to combine with the onion and garlic. Season with a few pinches of salt and pepper. Continue to sauté for 4 to 5 minutes.

Add the vegetable broth and another pinch of salt and pepper to the pot. Bring to a simmer. Reduce the heat to medium-low, and simmer for about 10 minutes, stirring frequently.

Pour in the cashew cream, the cheese and garlic powder. Stir to combine everything. Then simmer for another 2 to 3 minutes. Taste and adjust seasoning; I usually find I need more salt and pepper.

Serve immediately, topped with extra cheese, chives or green onions, if desired, and the mushroom "bacon."

Creamy Toscana Rigatoni

I used to be an endless soup, salad and breadsticks kind of gal. I spent many a day at the local Olive Garden®, because when you're there . . . well, you know the rest. This devilishly creamy soup was inspired by their Zuppa Toscana, traditionally made with potatoes, kale and sausage. I traded one carb for another and used pasta instead of potatoes. It has all the same flavors of the classic soup: the cheesiness, the creaminess, the sausage and the kale, with a touch of spice. This rigatoni will be a dish you go back to for seconds, thirds or maybe even fourths.

Serves 4

1 cup (146 g) raw cashews

1 cup (240 ml) almond milk or other nondairy milk

Salt and pepper, to taste

2 tbsp (30 ml) extra-virgin olive oil

4 cloves garlic, finely chopped

½ yellow onion, chopped

4 vegan sausages (I prefer Beyond Sausage Hot Italian)

6 cups (1.4 L) vegetable broth

16 oz (448 g) rigatoni

3 cups (200 g) kale, chopped

½ cup (50 g) vegan Parmesan (I prefer Follow Your Heart®)

Pinch of red pepper flakes, plus more for serving

Fresh basil, for serving (optional)

Soak the cashews in room-temperature water for 8 to 12 hours, or boil them for 15 to 20 minutes.

Make the cashew cream. Drain the soaked cashews, and add them to a blender with the milk and a pinch of salt and pepper. Blend on high, scraping down the sides as needed until the cashew cream is completely smooth. Set aside.

Make the soup. In a large pot over medium-high heat, heat the olive oil. Add the garlic and onion. Sauté, reducing the heat as needed, for 1 to 2 minutes, or until the onion is translucent. Crumble the sausages, and add them to the pot. Brown the sausages for 4 to 5 minutes. Transfer the sausage crumbles, garlic and onion to a bowl, and set aside.

Pour the vegetable broth into the pot, and increase the heat to medium-high. Bring to a simmer, then pour the rigatoni into the pot. Season with a pinch of salt and pepper. Stir, and make sure the rigatoni is submerged in the broth. Simmer the rigatoni, stirring occasionally, until it is al dente and most of the liquid has been absorbed, 15 to 16 minutes.

Once the pasta is al dente, add the kale to the pot and stir. The kale will begin to wilt. Allow it to cook for about 1 minute. Pour the cashew cream into the pot, as well as the Parmesan and another pinch of salt and pepper. Stir to combine, making sure the pasta is all coated in the sauce.

Return the sausage crumbles, garlic and onion to the pot, and toss to combine. Sprinkle with a pinch of red pepper flakes. Stir. Taste and adjust seasonings.

Serve immediately with extra red pepper flakes or basil, if desired.

Mouth-Watering Red Curry Ramen

My kid has a current but lengthy obsession with ramen. It's all she wants to eat at the moment. While I am also haunted by my cravings for any Asian noodles, I get bored with the same thing over and over again. So, after one hundred days in a row of having to make very plain and basic ramen, I decided to switch it up a bit. Most nights I dream of this red curry ramen and I walking hand in hand along the beach. It is everything I want in a ramen: a little spicy, a tad bit creamy, a smidge of sweetness and tartness. You're gonna love it, too.

Serves 4

6 oz (170 g) ramen noodles (about 2 packages)

1 tbsp (15 ml) sesame oil

2 shallots, diced

6 cloves garlic, chopped

1 (1-inch [2.5-cm]) piece fresh ginger, grated

2 tbsp (32 g) vegan red curry paste

2 tbsp (32 g) tomato paste

4 cups (960 ml) vegetable broth

1 (13.5-oz [399-ml]) can coconut cream or full-fat coconut milk

1 tbsp (15 ml) soy sauce

1 tbsp (15 ml) agave syrup, plus more as needed

1 tbsp (15 ml) rice wine vinegar, plus more as needed

Salt, to taste

Mushrooms, cilantro, sesame seeds, kimchi and/or green onions, for topping (optional)

In a large soup pot, cook the ramen according to package directions, then drain.

In the same pot over medium-high heat, heat the sesame oil. Add the shallots, garlic and ginger. Sauté, reducing the heat as needed, until the shallots are translucent, 2 to 3 minutes. Add the red curry paste and tomato paste to the pot. Whisk to combine everything, and simmer for about 1 minute.

Add the vegetable broth, coconut cream, soy sauce, agave, rice wine vinegar and a pinch of salt. Whisk to combine, and bring to a simmer. Reduce the heat to medium-low, and simmer for about 15 minutes to develop the flavors. Taste and adjust seasonings, adding more salt, vinegar or agave if needed. Turn off the heat.

Add the ramen noodles to the broth, and stir to combine. Let the ramen sit in the broth for 1 to 2 minutes.

Serve immediately with any toppings you want.

Simple Lemongrass Noodle Soup

Several times a month, I feel pretty sick. Whilst I should probably see a doctor about that, for the time being, this lemongrass noodle soup comes in handy. It is deep down comfort food, one that warms your whole body and makes you instantly feel better. The ease with which you can make this soup makes this a task you can definitely handle even when you are under the weather. And while the world is a crumbling sarcophagus of misery, there is always this soup.

Serves 4

1 (12-oz [336-g]) package rice noodles

1 tbsp (15 ml) vegetable oil

4 cloves garlic, chopped

1 large carrot, diced

1 stalk celery, diced

1 (1-inch [2.5-cm]) piece fresh ginger, grated

4 tbsp (20 g) vegan prepared lemongrass, or 1 stalk lemongrass, smashed

2 dried red chilies

1 tsp coriander

6 cups (1.4 L) vegetable broth

½ cup (120 ml) coconut cream or full-fat coconut milk

2 tbsp (30 ml) soy sauce

1 tbsp (14 g) vegan light brown sugar

1 tbsp (15 ml) lime juice

Salt, to taste

Broccoli, mushrooms and/or bok choy, for serving (optional)

Fresh cilantro and/or green onions, for serving (optional)

In a large pot, cook the noodles according to package directions, then drain and set aside.

In the same pot over medium-high heat, heat the vegetable oil. Add the garlic, carrot, celery and ginger. Sauté, reducing the heat as needed, for 1 to 2 minutes. Add the lemongrass, red chilies and coriander. Toss to combine, and sauté for another minute.

Add the vegetable broth, coconut cream, soy sauce, brown sugar, lime juice and a pinch of salt. Whisk to combine. Bring to a simmer, reduce the heat to medium-low, and simmer for 12 to 15 minutes. If you used a stalk of lemongrass, remove that now. Taste and adjust seasonings. It may need more salt.

Return the noodles to the pot, and stir to combine. Let it simmer for another minute. Then turn off the heat. If you are adding vegetables, do that now, and let them steam in the soup for 4 to 5 minutes.

Serve the soup with cilantro and green onions, if desired.

*See photo on page 72.

Crispy Shallot and Garlic Chili Oil Udon Noodles

This is the dish you want to have on hand for all those late-night noodle cravings. I've made this recipe a lot, and I had honestly forgotten how mind-bogglingly flavorful these noodles are. They are so simple; they don't seem like much. However, one taste of them and you'll be a lifetime member of the Chili Oil Udon Noodle Club (you'll receive your membership card in the mail in one to two weeks!). These noodles make everything better, and they literally take 5 minutes to make.

Serves 4

1 (14-oz [392-g]) package udon noodles

1 green onion, chopped

¼ cup (4 g) fresh cilantro, chopped

2 large shallots, sliced

8 cloves garlic, chopped

½ tsp fresh ginger, grated

1 tbsp (5 g) chili flakes

1 tbsp (15 ml) soy sauce

1 tbsp (15 ml) rice wine vinegar

1 tsp cane sugar

½ tsp salt

½ cup (120 ml) vegetable oil

Cook the udon noodles according to package directions. I usually use the microwave method. Put them in a heat-proof bowl when they are done. Add the green onion and cilantro to the bowl with the udon noodles.

In a small heat-proof bowl, combine the shallots, garlic, ginger, chili flakes, soy sauce, rice wine vinegar, sugar and salt. Toss to combine, and set aside.

In a small saucepan over medium-high heat, heat the oil until it begins to form tiny bubbles, 3 to 5 minutes. Pour the hot oil slowly into the bowl with the shallots and garlic. Stir and let sit for about 5 minutes.

Pour the shallot, garlic and chili oil over the udon noodles. Toss to coat the noodles in the chili oil. Serve immediately.

*See photo on page 72.

Terry's Tikka Masala-Inspired Tofu

I have talked many a person over the years into trying Indian food, but no one held on to it, embraced it and absolutely fell head over heels in love with Indian food more than my partner, Terry. So, this Indian-inspired dish is for him. I'm passionate about him, and he's passionate about Indian food. This simplified tikka masala is a one-pot meal, and tofu replaces the chicken. If you are looking to start trying some Indian-inspired flavors, you have come to the right place. This one is phenomenal.

Serves 4

1 (15-oz [425-g]) block extra-firm or super-firm tofu, drained and pressed

1 (13.5-oz [399-ml]) can coconut cream or full-fat coconut milk, divided

4 cloves garlic, chopped

1½ tsp (3 g) garam masala

1 tsp ground ginger

1 tsp salt

½ tsp cumin

½ tsp turmeric

½ tsp chili powder

½ cup (68 g) cornstarch

¼ cup (60 ml) vegetable oil

2 tbsp (28 g) vegan butter

1 small sweet onion, diced

1 tsp coriander

1 (15-oz [425-g]) can tomato sauce

1 tsp vegan light brown sugar

Pinch of red pepper flakes

Rice and naan, for serving

Fresh cilantro, for serving (optional)

Cut the block of tofu into cubes (for extra-firm) or break into chunks (for super-firm). Set aside.

In a large mixing bowl, whisk together 1 cup (240 ml) of the coconut cream, reserving the rest for later. Add the garlic, garam masala, ginger, salt, cumin, turmeric and chili powder. Add the tofu to the mixing bowl, and toss to coat in the marinade. Let the tofu sit in the marinade for at least 10 minutes or up to an hour.

After the tofu has marinated, remove the tofu from the marinade with a slotted spoon, and reserve the marinade. Put the tofu into a medium mixing bowl. Sprinkle the tofu with the cornstarch, and toss to coat completely.

In a large nonstick pot or skillet over medium-high heat, heat the vegetable oil. When the oil is hot, add about half of the tofu, and fry on each side for 2 to 3 minutes, or until the tofu is brown and firm. Reduce the heat as needed. Remove the tofu from the pot, and repeat with the remaining tofu. Place all the tofu into a bowl, and set aside.

Wipe out the excess oil from the pot. Add the butter, and heat over medium heat. Once the butter is melted, add the onion and coriander. Sauté for 1 to 2 minutes, or until the onion is translucent.

Add the reserved marinade, the remaining coconut cream, the tomato sauce, brown sugar and red pepper flakes. Whisk to combine. Reduce the heat to low, and simmer for 10 to 15 minutes. Taste and adjust seasoning. Add the fried tofu back to the pot with the sauce, and simmer for 2 to 3 minutes.

Serve immediately with rice and naan. Topped with cilantro, if desired.

Satisfying
PASTA BOWLS

I strongly believe that pasta is one of the all-time greatest inventions in the history of the universe. We all know pasta is a quintessential comfort food. There are so many different ways to make pasta, and I seriously adore them all. No jokes here. I haven't met too many human beings who don't enjoy pasta one way or another, so no matter what recipes you frequent in this chapter, they are sure to please you and your favorite people.

In the mood for creamy pasta? Hit up the Creamy AF Mushroom Linguine (page 83) or the One-Pot Broccoli Mac and Cheeze (page 86). Craving a savory delight? Check out the White Wine Garlic-Stuffed Shells (page 89) or the Zesty Pistachio Pesto Pappardelle (page 82). If you're craving an Asian-inspired noodle bowl, go for the Fried Garlic Dan Dan Noodles (page 94) or the Spicy Peanut Veggie Soba Noodle Salad (page 96). If you still fan-girl over any of your past pasta experiences, you are in for a treat with this chapter, my friend.

Easy Fresh "Egg" Noodles

Contrary to popular belief, most boxed dried pastas you find in the grocery store are, in fact, vegan. So you may be covered in that area. What I've been missing, though, are some delicious, chewy egg noodles. This super simple fresh "egg" noodle recipe is awesome. It is quick to throw together and perfect for a creamy stroganoff, a hearty "chicken" noodle soup or the perfect kugel.

Serves 4

1½ cups (185 g) all-purpose flour, plus more for dusting

1 tsp salt

½ cup (120 ml) vegan egg

2 tbsp (30 ml) nondairy milk

To a food processor, add the flour and salt.

In a small mixing bowl, whisk together the vegan egg and milk.

Turn on the food processor, and while the food processor is going, start streaming in the egg and milk mixture. Let the processor continue until the mixture comes together and forms a dough ball. Turn the dough out onto a floured surface. If the pasta dough is still sticky, add a bit more flour. Knead the dough until it is no longer sticky. Let the dough rest for about an hour. You can just let it rest at room temperature, covered with a kitchen towel.

When ready to make the pasta, roll it out, using a rolling pin or a pasta sheet roller. You want it to be about ⅛ inch (3 mm) thick. Shape the noodles however you want, in long strips or short noodles.

Bring a pot of salted water to a boil, and boil the noodles for 2 to 3 minutes, or until al dente.

Serve with some salt and butter, a little vegan Parmesan and lemon juice, or your favorite pasta sauce.

Zesty Pistachio Pesto Pappardelle

When I was about 10 years old, I tried pesto for the first time. Up to that point, my parents and brother would constantly try to get me to taste it, but I was a basic salt and buttered noodles kind of gal, and refused. We bought premade pesto from the store, and I finally gave in and stuck a piece of crusty bread into the tub of pesto. Well, the rest is history, because I was forever changed for the better and have been obsessively making different pesto recipes ever since. This pistachio pesto is one of the best, so enjoy like a 10-year-old trying pesto for the first time.

Serves 4

1 batch Easy Fresh "Egg" Noodles (page 81)

3 cups (72 g) fresh basil

½ cup (50 g) vegan Parmesan, plus more for topping

⅓ cup (41 g) roasted, salted pistachios, shells removed

4 cloves garlic

½ tsp salt

½ tsp black pepper

1 tsp lemon zest

½ cup (120 ml) extra-virgin olive oil

Prep the Easy Fresh "Egg" Noodles, and cut the noodles into long strips that are about ½ inch (1.3 cm) wide and resemble pappardelle noodles.

Boil the noodles, and drain when al dente.

In a food processor, add the basil, Parmesan, pistachios, garlic, salt, pepper and lemon zest. Start the food processor, and begin to stream in the olive oil as the food processor is going. Process until all of the olive oil is incorporated and the pesto is smooth. Taste and adjust seasonings.

Heat a large nonstick skillet over medium-high heat. Add the pesto, and simmer for about 1 minute, reducing the heat as needed. Add the cooked noodles to the skillet, and toss to coat. Let cook for just another minute to make sure everything is hot.

Serve immediately with extra Parmesan and red pepper flakes on top, if desired.

*See photo on page 80.

Creamy AF Mushroom Linguine

In January 2022, my favorite people and I ate at Catch in Las Vegas. While you may think this is obviously a seafood-heavy restaurant, you are both correct and incorrect. They have lots of vegan options, and we tried this absolutely perfect creamy mushroom pasta. This recipe is inspired by that. I, of course, don't know exactly how they made it. But, it was a blended mushroom sauce, not just mushrooms tossed with pasta. I did my best here, and frankly, my best tastes pretty darn good.

Serves 4

1½ lb (680 g) mushrooms, sliced (I prefer a mix of baby bella, shiitake and button)

10 cloves garlic, roughly chopped

2 shallots, diced

¼ cup (60 ml) extra-virgin olive oil

Salt and pepper, to taste

12 oz (340 g) linguine

1 cup (240 ml) reserved pasta water

1 cup (240 ml) vegan whipping cream

½ tsp lemon zest

1 tsp lemon juice

¼ cup (15 g) fresh parsley

½ cup (50 g) vegan Parmesan, plus more for serving

Preheat the oven to 400°F (204°C).

Put the mushrooms, garlic and shallots on a large baking sheet. Drizzle the olive oil over the vegetables. Sprinkle with a few pinches of salt and pepper. Toss to coat everything evenly. Roast for 20 minutes, toss and roast for another 15 to 20 minutes, or until the mushrooms are nice and brown.

Cook the linguine according to package directions. Make sure to reserve at least 1 cup (240 ml) of pasta water, draining the rest once the pasta is al dente.

While the pasta cooks, in a blender or food processor, add half of the mushrooms, garlic and shallots. Add the whipping cream, lemon zest, lemon juice, parsley and a pinch of salt and pepper. Blend, scraping down the sides as needed, until the mixture is smooth.

Heat a large nonstick skillet over medium heat. Add the mushroom sauce. Stir and bring to a simmer. Reduce the heat to low.

Once the linguine is done, add it to the skillet with about ½ cup (120 ml) of the reserved pasta water and the Parmesan. Toss to coat, adding more reserved pasta water as needed, until the pasta sauce is super creamy. Taste and adjust seasonings.

Scoop the remaining mushrooms, garlic and shallots into the skillet, and toss to combine. Serve immediately with more Parmesan, if desired.

*See photo on page 78.

Cheezy Cacio e Pepe Ravioli

Sometimes the simplest and easiest recipe ends up being the most satisfying. This ravioli sticks with the vibe of cacio e pepe, which translates simply to "cheese and pepper." This dish is painless and cost-effective. It also just might be the cheesiest, most delicious ravioli you will ever put in your mouth. I mean, little pasta dough pockets filled with tofu cheesiness. Come on! Top these bad boys with fresh cracked black pepper and savor every bite.

Serves 6

Filling

½ block (about 8 oz [225 g]) extra-firm tofu, drained and pressed

1 tsp extra-virgin olive oil

1 shallot, roughly chopped

1 clove garlic

2 tbsp (30 ml) lemon juice

1 tbsp (5 g) nutritional yeast

1 tsp white miso paste

¼ tsp salt

½ tsp black pepper

⅓ cup (33 g) vegan Parmesan

For the Ravioli

2 batches Easy Fresh "Egg" Noodles (page 81)

¼ cup (54 g) vegan butter

½ tsp fresh cracked black pepper, plus more for topping

¼ to ½ cup (60 to 120 ml) reserved pasta water

¼ cup (25 g) vegan Parmesan, plus more for topping

Make the filling. In a food processor, combine the tofu, olive oil, shallot, garlic, lemon juice, nutritional yeast, miso paste, salt and pepper. Process, scraping down the sides as needed, until the mixture is smooth, 1 to 2 minutes. Put the mixture in a medium mixing bowl, and stir in the Parmesan. Put the mixture in the refrigerator until you're ready to make the ravioli.

Make the ravioli. Make two batches of the Easy Fresh "Egg" Noodles. Once you get to the rolling out step, cut the dough into four equal pieces. Roll out each piece of dough to about a 6 x 12–inch (15 x 30–cm) rectangle that is about ⅛ inch (3 mm) thick.

Taking two pieces of the rolled-out pasta sheets, place about 1 to 2 teaspoons (5 to 10 g) of the filling all along the two sheets of pasta about an inch (2.5 cm) apart, creating two rows on each sheet, a top and a bottom row.

Take the remaining two sheets of pasta, and lay one on top of each of the pasta sheets with the filling. Gently press the top sheets of pasta down around each pocket of filling. Using a ravioli cutter or knife, cut out each individual ravioli.

Bring a large pot of salted water to a boil. Drop in the ravioli, and boil for 2 to 3 minutes, or until they float to the surface and are al dente.

Meanwhile, in a large nonstick skillet over medium heat, heat the butter. Once the butter is melted, add the black pepper. Simmer for 1 to 2 minutes.

When the ravioli are done cooking, reserve ¼ to ½ cup (60 to 120 ml) of pasta water. Remove the ravioli from the pot, and add them straight to the skillet with the butter and pepper. Add in the Parmesan and about ¼ cup (60 ml) of the reserved pasta water. Toss to coat the ravioli, and add a little more reserved pasta water if you need it to be a little saucier.

Serve immediately, topped with extra black pepper and Parmesan, if desired.

*See photo on page 78.

Will's Chick'n Parmesan Lasagna Roll-Ups

I really enjoy marrying two dishes together, so I thought, "Why not pair chicken parmesan and lasagna?" It turns out that they make quite a tasty team. If you don't know Julie yet, she's my BFF, the blog manager for Rabbit and Wolves and second photographer for this cookbook. This recipe is named after her husband, Will, who is a big fan of lasagna. Creamy on the inside and crunchy and cheezy on the outside, you will love these roll-ups.

Yields 12 roll-ups

Tofu "Ricotta"
½ block (about 8 oz [226 g]) extra-firm tofu, drained and pressed

1 tsp extra-virgin olive oil

2 cloves garlic

1 tbsp (5 g) nutritional yeast

2 tbsp (30 ml) lemon juice

¼ tsp salt

Pinch of black pepper

½ cup (50 g) vegan Parmesan

Marinara Chick'n
4 oz (113 g) soy curls, soaked and drained

3 tbsp (45 ml) extra-virgin olive oil

4 cloves garlic, finely chopped

1 tsp vegan chicken seasoning or bouillon

1 cup (240 ml) marinara sauce of choice

For the Roll-Ups
9 lasagna sheets, cooked

2 cups (480 ml) marinara sauce

2 cups (224 g) vegan mozzarella

½ cup (54 g) plain vegan breadcrumbs

½ tsp dried oregano

½ tsp dried basil

Pinch of salt and pepper

⅓ cup (33 g) vegan Parmesan

Preheat the oven to 425°F (218°C).

Make the tofu "ricotta." In a food processor, add the tofu, olive oil, garlic, nutritional yeast, lemon juice, salt and pepper. Process, scraping down the sides as needed, until the mixture is smooth, 1 to 2 minutes. Put the "ricotta" in a bowl, add the Parmesan and stir to combine. Put the "ricotta" in the refrigerator until ready to use.

Make the marinara chick'n. Chop the soy curls into small chunks.

In a large nonstick skillet over medium-high heat, heat the olive oil. Add the soy curls and garlic, and sauté for 2 to 3 minutes. Add the chicken seasoning, and toss to combine. Sauté, reducing the heat as needed, until the soy curls are brown and firm, 8 to 10 minutes. Pour in the marinara sauce, and toss to coat the soy curls. Simmer for 1 minute, then turn off the heat.

Put together the lasagna roll-ups. Lay one lasagna sheet out on a flat surface, and spread about 2 tablespoons (31 g) of the "ricotta" mixture over the whole sheet. Spread out about 2 tablespoons (17 g) of the marinara chick'n over the sheet. Roll the lasagna sheet up into a spiral. Repeat with all 9 lasagna sheets.

Spread 1 cup (240 ml) of marinara sauce into the bottom of a 9 x 13–inch (23 x 33–cm) baking dish. Lay all the lasagna roll-ups in the baking dish. Top with the remaining 1 cup (240 ml) of marinara sauce, and spread it out evenly over the roll-ups. Top that with the vegan mozzarella.

In a small mixing bowl, stir together the breadcrumbs, dried oregano, dried basil, salt and pepper. Sprinkle the breadcrumb mixture evenly over the top of the roll-ups. Sprinkle the vegan Parmesan on top of the breadcrumbs. Bake for 18 to 22 minutes, or until the breadcrumbs are golden brown.

Serve immediately. These are perfect to make ahead. You can make the roll-ups and put them in the baking dish. Put them in the refrigerator overnight, then add the toppings and bake when ready.

*See photo on page 87.

One-Pot Broccoli Mac and Cheeze

There was a time in the '90s when I thought nothing was more brilliant than Kraft® Deluxe Cheddar Broccoli Macaroni & Cheese. When grocery shopping with my dad on a pretty regular basis, that is all I would ask for. He would talk to me about the most cost-effective macaroni and cheese, and I would talk to him about how I just wanted the freaking mac and cheese with broccoli. This recipe is so reminiscent of that sweet golden, saucy, cheesy goodness. It's all made in one pot, too!

Serves 4

1 tbsp (15 ml) extra-virgin olive oil

4 cloves garlic, roughly chopped

1 medium head broccoli, cut into florets

2½ cups (600 ml) oat milk or other nondairy milk

3 cups (720 ml) water

1½ tsp (9 g) salt

½ tsp black pepper

1 tsp garlic powder

16 oz (454 g) pasta shells or macaroni

8 oz (226 g) vegan Cheddar-style shreds

In a large pot over medium-high heat, heat the olive oil. Add the garlic and sauté, reducing the heat as needed, for about 1 minute. Add the broccoli to the pot, and toss to combine with the garlic. Sauté for about 1 minute.

Add the nondairy milk, water, salt, pepper and garlic powder. Stir to combine and bring to a simmer. Pour in the pasta, stir and make sure the pasta is as submerged in the liquid as possible. Reduce the heat to medium, and let the pasta simmer until al dente and most of the liquid has been absorbed, stirring frequently, 15 to 20 minutes.

Once the pasta is cooked, add the Cheddar to the pot, and stir until the cheese melts. Taste and adjust seasonings.

White Wine Garlic-Stuffed Shells

My brother will tell you a tale of how, when I was a kid, I would tell everyone I didn't like "things stuffed with things." I thought I hated ravioli, tortellini and shells. Of course, I was just afraid to try things. Now, I obviously love stuffed pastas. These stuffed shells are filled with a garlicky "ricotta" and baked with the most incredible garlic and white wine béchamel sauce. They get bubbly and cheesy. Served with a good Caesar salad on the side, these shells are the "stuff" dreams are made of.

Serves 6

8 oz (226 g) jumbo pasta shells

8 oz (226 g) vegan ricotta, home-made tofu "ricotta" (page 85) or store-bought

1 cup (112 g) vegan mozzarella-style shreds

1 tsp dried basil

1 tsp dried oregano

1 tsp garlic powder

Salt and pepper, to taste

¼ cup (54 g) vegan butter

6 cloves garlic, finely chopped

¼ cup (31 g) all-purpose flour

3 cups (720 ml) nondairy milk

1 cup (240 ml) vegan white wine

2 sprigs fresh thyme

1 cup (100 g) vegan Parmesan, divided

Make the pasta. Cook the pasta shells according to package directions, and drain when al dente. Let the shells cool to room temperature so you can handle them. I like to toss them with a little olive oil so they don't stick together as they cool.

While the pasta cooks, make the filling. In a small mixing bowl, combine the ricotta, mozzarella, dried basil, dried oregano, garlic powder and a pinch of salt and pepper. Stir together, then set aside.

Preheat the oven to 350°F (176°C).

Make a bechamel sauce. In a large nonstick skillet over medium-high heat, heat the butter. Add the garlic and sauté, reducing the heat to medium, for about 2 minutes. Add the flour, and whisk to combine and make a roux. Let it simmer for a minute.

Add the milk, white wine and a pinch of salt and pepper. Whisk to fully combine and make sure there are no lumps of roux left. Add the thyme sprigs and stir. Bring to a simmer, reduce the heat to medium-low, and let it simmer for 6 to 8 minutes. The sauce will thicken, and you want the wine taste to cook off a bit. Add ½ cup (50 g) of the Parmesan to the sauce, and let it melt. Taste and adjust seasonings. Remove the thyme sprigs.

Pour half of the béchamel sauce into the bottom of a 9 x 13–inch (23 x 33–cm) baking dish.

Take one of the jumbo pasta shells, and fill it with about 2 teaspoons (9 g) of the "ricotta" filling. Repeat with all of the shells, and lay them into the baking dish on top of the béchamel.

Pour the remaining béchamel sauce over the top of the shells, and then sprinkle with the remaining ½ cup (50 g) of Parmesan. Bake for 15 to 20 minutes, or until the dish is hot and bubbly. Serve immediately.

Spicy Greek Meatballs and Spaghetti

I don't mean to brag or anything, but I was just on the most awesome trip in Greece. It was a food-centric itinerary and designed just for Rabbit and Wolves. So, needless to say, I fell in love with all the Greek flavors. Greeks love their fresh produce, so for this recipe, I added cucumbers, red onion and olives into the actual meatballs. The spaghetti has tomatoes, artichokes and more olives. Plus, some vegan feta that makes a lovely creamy sauce. It is salty, a little spicy and super uniquely flavored as far as meatballs go.

Serves 6

"Meat" Balls

½ red onion, roughly chopped

4 cloves garlic

½ cup (90 g) Kalamata olives, pitted

½ cup (51 g) cucumber, roughly chopped

2 tbsp (14 g) flax meal

3 tbsp (45 ml) water

1 lb (454 g) vegan ground beef

1 tbsp (15 ml) extra-virgin olive oil

1 cup (108 g) plain vegan bread-crumbs

¼ cup (15 g) fresh parsley, finely chopped

½ tsp dried oregano

1 tsp salt

¼ tsp red pepper flakes

Preheat the oven to 375°F (190°C). Spray the inside of a 9 x 9–inch (23 x 23–cm) baking dish with nonstick spray.

Make the "meat" balls. In a food processor, add the red onion, garlic, olives and cucumber. Pulse until all the vegetables are very finely chopped. Set aside.

Make a flax egg. In a small bowl, whisk together the flax meal and water. Let sit for 2 to 3 minutes to thicken.

Meanwhile, put the ground beef in a large mixing bowl. Scoop the processed vegetables into the bowl.

Add the flax egg to the bowl, as well as the olive oil, breadcrumbs, parsley, dried oregano, salt and red pepper flakes. Stir together with a wooden spoon or rubber spatula. Once the mixture starts to come together, mix the rest of the way by hand to make sure everything is fully combined.

Scoop out 1 to 2 tablespoons (14 to 28 g) of the meatball mixture, and roll it into a ball. Place it in the prepared baking dish. Repeat with all of the meatball mixture, and place them all right up against each other in the baking dish. You should get 24 to 30 meatballs. Bake for 20 to 25 minutes, or until the meatballs are brown and cooked through.

(continued)

Spaghetti

1 lb (454 g) spaghetti

¼ to ½ cup (60 to 120 ml) reserved pasta water

1 tbsp (15 ml) extra-virgin olive oil

6 cloves garlic, finely chopped

1 tsp dried oregano

1 pint (298 g) grape tomatoes, roasted or fresh

1 (14-oz [397-g]) can artichoke hearts, drained and chopped

1 cup (180 g) Kalamata olives, chopped

Salt and red pepper flakes, to taste

4 oz (113 g) vegan feta, plus more for topping (I prefer Violife)

½ cup (120 ml) vegan heavy cream or nondairy milk of choice

Fresh parsley, chopped, for topping (optional)

Make the spaghetti. While the meatballs bake, cook the spaghetti according to package directions, reserving ¼ to ½ cup (60 to 120 ml) of the pasta water. Drain when al dente.

In a large nonstick skillet over medium-high heat, heat the olive oil. Add the garlic and dried oregano. Sauté, reducing the heat as needed, for about 2 minutes. Add the tomatoes, artichoke hearts and olives to the skillet, as well as a pinch of salt and red pepper flakes. Sauté for about 5 minutes. Add the vegan feta and vegan heavy cream to the skillet. Stir to combine, and let the vegan feta melt a bit.

Add the cooked spaghetti to the skillet, and pour in ¼ cup (60 ml) of the reserved pasta water. Toss the spaghetti in the skillet, and combine everything to make a creamy sauce. Add more pasta water if needed for a creamier texture. Add a few pinches of salt and red pepper flakes. Taste and adjust seasonings.

Once the meatballs are done, serve the spaghetti with some meatballs on top. Top with parsley and more vegan feta, if desired.

*See photo on page 88.

Fiery Green Curry Veggie Noodles

If you're in the mood for some *kick*, this is your dish. It has "fiery" in the title, so that gives you a clue into the flavor-packed recipe you'll be making. This creamy dish also provides a noodle extravaganza with not only spaghetti, but also healthier zucchini and butternut squash noodles mixed in as well. Honestly, the flavor is incredible, and you can customize the spice as needed.

Make it as punchy as you like by adding your desired amount of chili crisp on top.

Serves 4

6 oz (170 g) spaghetti

1 tbsp (15 ml) sesame oil

6 cloves garlic, grated

2 tsp (4 g) fresh ginger, grated

2 shallots, diced

2 tbsp (32 g) green curry paste

1 (13.5-oz [399-ml]) can full-fat coconut milk

2 cups (480 ml) vegetable broth

2 tbsp (28 g) vegan light brown sugar

2 tbsp (30 ml) soy sauce

2 tsp (10 ml) lime juice

1 tsp rice wine vinegar

Salt, to taste

Pinch of red pepper flakes

6 oz (170 g) zucchini noodles, cooked (frozen or homemade, see Note)

6 oz (170 g) butternut squash or sweet potato noodles, cooked (frozen or homemade, see Note)

¼ cup (4 g) fresh cilantro, chopped

1 green onion

Chili crisp or chili oil (page 94), for topping

Cook the spaghetti according to package directions, and drain when al dente.

Meanwhile, in a large nonstick skillet over medium-high heat, heat the sesame oil. Add the garlic, ginger and shallots. Sauté, reducing the heat as needed, until the shallots are translucent, about 2 minutes. Stir in the green curry paste, and sauté for another minute.

Add the coconut milk, vegetable broth, brown sugar, soy sauce, lime juice, rice wine vinegar, a pinch of salt and a pinch of red pepper flakes. Whisk to fully combine, making sure there are no lumps of curry paste. Bring to a simmer, then reduce the heat to medium-low, and let it simmer for 15 to 17 minutes, or until the sauce thickens slightly. Taste and adjust seasonings.

Add the spaghetti and veggie noodles to the skillet, and toss to coat them in the sauce. Let them simmer in the sauce for 1 to 2 minutes. Add the cilantro and green onion, and toss to combine.

Serve immediately with chili crisp or chili oil on top.

Note: You can buy premade vegetable noodles in the frozen section at the grocery store. Or make your own with a spiralizer. To cook the vegetable noodles, steam or sauté them for 2 to 3 minutes. You don't want to over cook them.

Fried Garlic Dan Dan Noodles

Dan dan noodles originate from China and consist of chili oil and minced pork over noodles. They are like nothing else, so I wanted to make a dan dan experience for all of us to enjoy. Tofu and mushrooms replace the ground pork, and the greatest homemade chili oil and some golden-brown fried garlic top these noodles.

Serves 4

Chili Oil (see Note)
8 cloves garlic, chopped
2 tbsp (10 g) red pepper flakes
2 tsp (5 g) sesame seeds
⅓ cup (80 ml) vegetable oil
1 tbsp (15 ml) sesame oil

Sauce
½ cup (120 ml) soy sauce
¼ cup (60 ml) hoisin sauce
2 tbsp (30 ml) rice wine vinegar
1 tbsp (15 ml) agave syrup
½ tsp five spice powder

"Meat"
1 shallot, diced
10 oz (280 g) mushrooms, finely chopped (such as baby bella or shiitake)
1 (15-oz [425-g]) block extra-firm tofu, drained and pressed

Noodles
8 oz (226 g) spaghetti or other long pasta
1½ cups (360 ml) vegetable broth
Green onions and peanuts, for garnish

Fried Garlic
½ cup (120 ml) vegetable oil
20 cloves garlic, thinly sliced

Make the chili oil. In a medium heat-proof bowl, combine the garlic, red pepper flakes and sesame seeds. Set aside.

In a small saucepan over medium-high heat, heat the vegetable and sesame oils until you see small bubbles forming. Turn off the heat, and pour the hot oil over the garlic, red pepper flakes and sesame seeds. Whisk to combine. Let the oil sit and cool for about 15 minutes.

Make the sauce. In a medium mixing bowl, whisk together the soy sauce, hoisin sauce, rice wine vinegar, agave and five spice powder. Set aside.

Make the "meat." In a large nonstick skillet over medium-high heat, heat about 1 tablespoon (15 ml) of the chili oil. Add the shallot and mushrooms. Sauté, reducing the heat as needed, for 5 to 6 minutes, or until the mushrooms have released their liquid and are starting to brown.

Crumble the block of tofu into the skillet using your hands. Break up any larger pieces with a wooden spoon. Stir the tofu in with the shallot and mushrooms, and sauté for 5 to 7 minutes, or until the tofu starts to brown. Pour half of the sauce over the tofu and mushrooms, and toss to combine. Reduce the heat to low, and let it simmer while you make the noodles.

Cook the noodles according to the package directions. Drain and add the noodles back to the pot you cooked them in, then pour in the vegetable broth and the remaining sauce. Heat the pot over medium-low, and simmer the noodles in the liquid for 2 to 3 minutes. Turn off the heat.

Make the fried garlic. In a small saucepan over medium-high heat, heat the vegetable oil. Once small bubbles form, add the sliced garlic. Fry for 1 to 3 minutes, reducing the heat as needed, until the garlic starts to brown. Remove the garlic from the oil with a slotted spoon.

To serve, divide the noodles into bowls, pouring some of the broth and sauce over the top. Spoon a quarter of the "meat" mixture on top of each bowl of noodles. Then drizzle with the chili oil. Top with green onions, peanuts and fried garlic.

Note: This recipe will make more chili oil than you need, so save any you have left.

Spicy Peanut Veggie Soba Noodle Salad

Most people have days burned into their memories, big important days. The day they got married, the day their kids were born. One of those days for me is the day I tried peanut sauce for the first time. As a kid, dipping fresh spring rolls into that peanut-y goodness, I was forever changed and wanted that sauce on *everything*. From then on, I tried to perfect my own recipe at home and have since added it to salads, pizzas, sandwiches and sushi. This recipe is a culmination of everything I learned and everything I love about peanut sauce.

Serves 4

Roasted Veggies
1 cup (220 g) baby corn, chopped
1 cup (98 g) snow peas
1 cup (91 g) broccoli florets
1 cup (149 g) diced sweet peppers
1 cup (128 g) chopped carrots
1 cup (70 g) sliced cabbage
4 cloves garlic, finely chopped
¼ cup (60 ml) vegetable oil
¼ cup (60 ml) soy sauce

Spicy Peanut Soba Noodles
8 oz (226 g) soba noodles
¼ cup (65 g) peanut butter
¼ cup (60 ml) soy sauce
¼ cup (60 ml) water
2 to 4 tbsp (30 to 60 ml) sriracha
2 tbsp (30 ml) agave syrup
1 tbsp (15 ml) sesame oil
1 tbsp (15 ml) lime juice
2 cloves garlic, finely chopped
Peanuts and fresh cilantro, for garnish

Preheat the oven to 375°F (190°C).

Make the roasted veggies. In a large mixing bowl, combine the baby corn, snow peas, broccoli, sweet peppers, carrots, cabbage and garlic. Drizzle the vegetable oil and soy sauce over the vegetables, and toss with a rubber spatula to coat.

Pour the vegetables onto a large baking sheet, and spread them out evenly with a spatula. Roast for 15 minutes, toss the vegetables, and roast for another 10 to 12 minutes, or until the vegetables are tender and starting to brown.

While the vegetables roast, cook the soba noodles according to package directions. Drain when they are done.

While the vegetables and soba noodles are cooking, make the spicy peanut sauce. In a large mixing bowl, whisk together the peanut butter, soy sauce, water and sriracha (depending on how spicy you like your food; I use 4 tablespoons [60 ml], but I do like spicy food). Whisk in the agave, sesame oil, lime juice and garlic. Set aside.

Add the noodles and vegetables to the bowl with the peanut sauce, and toss with tongs to fully combine everything.

You can serve this hot, with peanuts and cilantro on top. Or you can toss peanuts and cilantro into the dish, chill and serve cold.

*See photo on page 95.

Black Pepper Noodles with Miso Mushrooms

If you're in the mood for a savory, flavor-packed pasta recipe (I almost always am), you've come to the right place. Roasted mushrooms are tossed in a sweet and salty miso-based sauce, then tossed again with spicy, rich black pepper noodles. The combined flavors are just delightful. This is such a satisfying and enjoyable pasta dish. If anyone claims they don't like mushrooms, this may just be the recipe that converts them.

Serves 4

Miso Mushrooms
¼ cup (60 ml) vegetable oil

¼ cup (60 ml) full-fat coconut milk

2 tbsp (30 g) white miso paste

1 tbsp (15 ml) soy sauce

1 tbsp (15 ml) rice wine vinegar

1 tsp sesame oil

4 cloves garlic, minced

20 oz (560 g) mushrooms, chopped (such as baby bella mushrooms)

Black Pepper Noodles
8 oz (226 g) lo mein noodles or other long noodles

2 tbsp (16 g) cornstarch

¼ cup (60 ml) vegetable broth

⅓ cup (80 ml) soy sauce

3 tbsp (45 ml) rice wine vinegar

2 tbsp (30 ml) agave syrup

1½ tsp (3 g) black pepper

1 (1-inch [2.5-cm]) piece fresh ginger, peeled and grated

4 cloves garlic, finely chopped

Green onions, thinly sliced (optional)

Preheat the oven to 425°F (218°C).

Start the miso mushrooms. In a large mixing bowl, whisk together the vegetable oil, coconut milk, miso paste, soy sauce, rice wine vinegar, sesame oil and garlic until fully combined. Add the chopped mushrooms to the bowl, and toss the mushrooms with a rubber spatula in the sauce until they are evenly coated.

Pour the mushrooms onto a large baking sheet, and spread them out evenly with the spatula. Roast for 10 minutes, toss the mushrooms and roast for another 10 minutes, or until they are nice and brown. They will be juicy.

While the mushrooms roast, cook the noodles according to package directions. Drain when they are done.

Make the black pepper sauce. In a medium mixing bowl, whisk together the cornstarch and vegetable broth until fully combined, making sure no lumps of cornstarch remain. Add the soy sauce, rice wine vinegar, agave, black pepper, ginger and garlic. Whisk to combine everything fully with the cornstarch mixture. Set aside.

Once the noodles and mushrooms are done, heat a large nonstick skillet over medium-low heat. Add the black pepper sauce to the skillet, and heat, whisking constantly, until the sauce begins to thicken, 1 to 2 minutes.

Add the noodles to the skillet, and toss them with tongs to coat them in the sauce. Then add the mushrooms with all the juices to the skillet, and toss to combine everything.

Serve immediately with green onions, if desired.

*See photo on page 95.

Feast-Worthy
FARE

Delicious gathering-inspired food can make or break a festive get together. When you have many people of all different ages, tastes and backgrounds attempting to come together over a celebratory feast, it can be stressful to plan the menu around pleasing every single person. And that's even without bringing plant-based food into the mix. We all know that not everyone is open to eating vegan food, no matter how yummy it looks and smells. As soon as you say, "... and it's vegan!" Uncle Jimmy poo-poos the dish immediately because he tried tofu once in 1995 and didn't like the texture.

I'm particularly excited about sharing these recipes with you because each one will make even the Uncle Jimmys at your event enjoy this feast-worthy fare. The Cider-Braised Pot Roast (page 101) makes a great centerpiece for a delicious feast. The Crispy Herbed Sweet Potato Stacks (page 110) are a savory gift from the heavens. The Jagerschnitzel with Creamy Mushroom Gravy (page 106) will have Uncle Jimmy lapping up every last crumb. You can't go wrong with any of these crowd-pleasers.

Cider-Braised Pot Roast

This vegan pot roast is very easy, so don't be intimidated by the seitan-making process. The seitan is coated in mustard and maple syrup, and seared first. Then, it is braised nice and slow in apple cider and broth. It is the fall feast we have all been casting a spell for.

Serves 8

Seitan

4 tbsp (60 ml) extra-virgin olive oil, divided

8 oz (226 g) mushrooms, diced

6 cloves garlic, finely chopped

1½ cups (360 ml) vegetable broth

1 tbsp (15 ml) apple cider vinegar

2 tbsp (30 ml) maple syrup, divided

2 tbsp (30 ml) Dijon mustard, divided

2 tbsp (30 g) tahini

1 tsp liquid smoke

2½ cups (300 g) vital wheat gluten, plus more as needed

1½ tsp (4 g) onion powder

1½ tsp (9 g) salt

1 tsp dried sage

¼ tsp black pepper

Braising Liquid

1½ cups (360 ml) apple cider or apple juice

1½ cups (360 ml) vegetable broth

1 sweet onion, cut into chunks

2 apples, quartered (such as Honeycrisp)

8 oz (226 g) carrots, roughly chopped

2 stalks celery, cut into chunks

2 sprigs fresh thyme

2 sprigs fresh rosemary

Pinch of salt and pepper

Preheat the oven to 375°F (190°C).

Make the seitan. In a large nonstick skillet over medium-high heat, heat 1 tablespoon (15 ml) of the olive oil. Add the mushrooms and garlic. Sauté, reducing the heat as needed, until the mushrooms have released their liquid and the liquid has evaporated, 6 to 8 minutes. Scoop the mushrooms and garlic into a food processor, and pulse until the mushrooms look almost like a paste.

Scoop the mushroom mixture into a large mixing bowl. Add 2 tablespoons (30 ml) of the olive oil, the vegetable broth, apple cider vinegar, 1 tablespoon (15 ml) of the maple syrup, 1 tablespoon (15 ml) of the Dijon, the tahini and liquid smoke. Whisk to combine everything.

In a separate large mixing bowl, whisk together the vital wheat gluten, onion powder, salt, sage and pepper.

Pour the wet ingredients into the dry ingredients, and begin to stir together. Once the mixture starts to come together, knead it with your hands. Knead for 2 to 3 minutes, or until the mixture forms a smooth ball that is no longer sticky. If the ball is still sticky, add about 1 tablespoon (8 g) more of vital wheat gluten at a time until it is no longer sticky and it will stay together in a nice ball. Form the seitan into a roast shape, like a small log.

In a small mixing bowl, whisk together the remaining 1 tablespoon (15 ml) of maple syrup and 1 tablespoon (15 ml) of Dijon. Brush the whole outside of the seitan roast with the mixture.

In the nonstick skillet you used for the mushrooms, heat the remaining 1 tablespoon (15 ml) of olive oil over medium-high heat. Put the seitan roast into the skillet, and sear each side until it gets golden brown, 2 to 3 minutes per side. Turn off the heat.

Make the braising liquid. In a large pot with a lid, whisk together the apple cider and broth. Add the onion, apples, carrots, celery, thyme, rosemary and a pinch of salt and pepper.

Put the seitan roast into the braising liquid. Cover and bake for 1 hour, then flip the roast and bake for another 30 to 45 minutes, or until the seitan roast is nice and firm.

Let the roast cool for a few minutes, then slice and serve with some of the braising liquid as a jus, if desired.

"Honey"-Glazed Autumn Tofu

When starting the brainstorming for this book, I knew I wanted to do a celebratory foods chapter. I really wanted to make sure I included main protein dishes that anyone could make. A few of the main dishes are a little more involved and time-consuming. However, this tofu is so freaking easy. Anyone can throw this together and take it to a potluck or have people over and serve it with a few of the side dishes from this chapter. I promise if you serve this beautifully glazed tofu with some mac and greens, sweet potato stacks and Parker House rolls, everyone will leave happy, after having to loosen their belts, of course.

Serves 2

1 (15-oz [425-g]) block extra-firm tofu, drained and pressed

2 tbsp (30 ml) agave syrup

1 tbsp (15 ml) apple cider or apple juice

1 tbsp (14 g) vegan light brown sugar

2 tsp (10 ml) Dijon mustard

½ tsp smoked paprika

A few pinches of salt and pepper

Preheat the oven to 400°F (204°C). Line a large baking sheet with parchment paper or a silicone mat.

Cut the tofu block into two to three "steaks," just cutting through the side of the tofu and leaving it in large rectangles that are about ½ inch (1.3 cm) thick. Cut in a crisscross pattern, just the top of the "steak," making sure not to cut all the way through the tofu. Cut in a diagonal one way and then back the other way. Place the tofu "steaks" on the prepared baking sheet.

Make the glaze. In a small mixing bowl, whisk together the agave, apple cider, brown sugar, Dijon, smoked paprika and a pinch of salt and pepper.

Sprinkle the tofu "steaks" with another pinch of salt and pepper. Brush the tofu "steaks" on each side with some of the glaze, making sure to get into the cuts you made on the top. You want to use about half of it, reserving the rest for another glazing.

Bake for 15 minutes, then brush with the remaining glaze and spoon any glaze that has thickened and pooled around the tofu back onto the tofu. Bake for another 15 to 20 minutes, or until the tofu is firm and golden brown.

Serve immediately.

*See photo on page 100.

Smoky "Bacon" Mac and Greens

OK, so this is a bit of a riff on a recipe from one of my favorite chefs, Marcus Samuelsson. His restaurant Red Rooster in Harlem provided me with one of the best meals I've ever had. You are correct to guess that Red Rooster is not very vegan-friendly, but they do have one vegan main dish. It is a whole roasted cauliflower that is so good it will make you angry. Since I couldn't eat a lot of the sides, I wanted to try to make my own version of his mac and greens. I hope I did it justice.

Serves 6

Greens

1 tbsp (15 ml) extra-virgin olive oil

2 slices vegan bacon, diced (I prefer Sweet Earth® Benevolent Bacon)

2 tbsp (30 ml) soy sauce

1 tsp Dijon mustard

4 cloves garlic, roughly chopped

4 cups (680 g) collard greens

½ cup (120 ml) coconut milk

Salt and pepper, to taste

Topping

½ cup (28 g) panko breadcrumbs

½ tsp salt

¼ tsp black pepper

2 tbsp (12 g) vegan Parmesan

Preheat the oven to 375°F (190°C).

Make the greens. In a large pot over medium-high heat, heat the olive oil. Add the bacon, and sauté until it is brown, 2 to 3 minutes. Add the soy sauce and Dijon, and stir to combine with the bacon. Add the garlic, and sauté for 1 to 2 minutes, or until it is golden brown.

Add the collard greens, coconut milk and a pinch of salt and pepper. Stir, cover and simmer for 15 to 17 minutes, or until the greens are tender. Remove the collard greens from the pot, and put them in a bowl. Set aside.

Make the topping. In a small mixing bowl, stir together the panko breadcrumbs, salt, pepper and Parmesan. Set aside.

(continued)

Smoky "Bacon" Mac and Greens (Continued)

Pasta

8 oz (226 g) short pasta

¼ cup (54 g) vegan butter

1 shallot, finely chopped

2 cloves garlic, finely chopped

¼ cup (31 g) all-purpose flour

2 cups (480 ml) nondairy milk

½ cup (120 ml) vegan heavy whipping cream (or more non-dairy milk)

Salt and pepper, to taste

8 oz (226 g) vegan cheese (a mixture of mozzarella-style and Cheddar-style shreds)

½ tsp nutmeg

½ tsp dried mustard

Make the pasta. Cook the pasta according to package directions. Drain when al dente.

In the same pot you used to cook the collard greens, heat the butter over medium heat. Once the butter is melted, add the shallot and garlic. Sauté, reducing the heat as needed, until the shallot is translucent, 1 to 2 minutes. Add the flour to the pot, and whisk to combine with the butter to make a roux.

Pour in the milk, heavy whipping cream and a pinch of salt and pepper. Whisk to combine with the roux, making sure there are no lumps of roux left. Bring to a simmer, reduce the heat to medium-low and let the sauce simmer until it thickens, 3 to 4 minutes.

Add the cheese, nutmeg, dried mustard and another pinch of salt and pepper to the pot. Whisk together, and continue to whisk until the cheese melts into the sauce, 2 to 3 minutes. Taste the sauce and adjust seasonings. Add the pasta and collard greens to the pot with the sauce, and stir to combine.

Pour the mac and greens into a 9 x 13–inch (23 x 33–cm) baking dish. Smooth out evenly with a rubber spatula. Sprinkle the topping over the mac and greens, and bake for 10 to 15 minutes, or until the top is golden brown. If you want to brown the top a little more, broil on high for 2 to 3 minutes—just make sure to keep your eyes on it.

Let sit for about 5 minutes, then serve.

Jagerschnitzel with Creamy Mushroom Gravy

Having an extensive German background, I grew up eating a decent amount of jagerschnitzel. Jagerschnitzel, as I am sure you know, is a fried thin slice of meat covered with a mushroom gravy. Instead of meat, I use thin cauliflower steaks. It satisfies that schnitzel craving perfectly.

Serves 4

Schnitzel

1 large head cauliflower

1 cup (240 ml) nondairy milk

1 tsp apple cider vinegar

¾ cup (94 g) all-purpose flour

½ cup (68 g) cornstarch

1 tsp salt, divided

1½ cups (162 g) plain vegan breadcrumbs

Pinch of black pepper

Vegetable oil, for frying

Gravy

1 tbsp (15 ml) extra-virgin olive oil

4 cloves garlic, finely chopped

8 oz (226 g) mushrooms, sliced

Salt and pepper, to taste

2 tbsp (28 g) vegan butter

2 tbsp (16 g) all-purpose flour

1½ cups (360 ml) vegetable broth

½ tsp organic cane sugar

½ tsp dried thyme

½ tsp dried rosemary

½ tsp dried sage

Preheat the oven to 425° (218°C).

Make the schnitzel. Cut the cauliflower into two to three large "steaks" that will hold together. Gather three medium mixing bowls. In the first one, whisk together the milk and apple cider vinegar. In the second one, whisk together the flour, cornstarch and ½ teaspoon of salt. In the third bowl, stir together the breadcrumbs, remaining ½ teaspoon of salt and the pepper.

Take one of the cauliflower "steaks," and dip it into the milk mixture, then put it into the bowl with the flour and cornstarch. Coat completely, then put it back into the milk mixture, then put it into the breadcrumbs and coat completely.

In a large nonstick skillet over medium-high heat, heat ¼ to ½ inch (3 mm to 1.3 cm) of vegetable oil. Fry the cauliflower "steaks," reducing the heat as needed, for 2 to 3 minutes per side or until they are golden brown. Place the cauliflower "steaks" on a large baking sheet.

Finish cooking the cauliflower in the oven; this will help cook the cauliflower all the way through. Bake the cauliflower for 5 to 7 minutes, or until they are crispy on the outside, but tender inside.

While the cauliflower bakes, make the gravy. In a large nonstick skillet over medium-high heat, heat the olive oil. Add the garlic and mushrooms, and sauté, reducing the heat as needed, until the mushrooms have released their liquid and start to brown, 5 to 7 minutes. Season with a pinch of salt and pepper, then transfer the mixture to a bowl and set aside.

Reduce the heat to medium, and add the butter to the skillet. Once the butter is melted, add the flour and whisk to combine, making a roux. Pour the vegetable broth into the skillet, and whisk to combine, making sure there are no lumps of roux left. Bring the broth to a simmer, and let it thicken, 2 to 3 minutes.

Add the sugar, thyme, rosemary, sage and a few pinches of salt and pepper. Whisk to combine. Taste and adjust seasoning. Scoop the mushrooms back into the gravy, and stir to combine. Turn off the heat.

Serve the cauliflower "steaks" with the mushroom gravy on top.

*See photo on page 105.

Cheezy Caramelized Onion Potato au Gratin

The terror of using a mandoline is not lost on me. I am, in fact, missing no less than two tips of my fingers due to my unearned confidence when it comes to using a mandoline. However, I would like to say, if ever there was a recipe to risk injuring yourself making, this would be the one. The sweetness of the caramelized onions, the cheezy, creamy sauce, those ultra-thinly sliced potatoes. Yeah, this is the one.

Serves 6

1 tbsp (15 ml) extra-virgin olive oil

1 large sweet onion, thinly sliced

1 tbsp (15 ml) agave syrup

Salt and pepper, to taste

3 tbsp (42 g) vegan butter

3 tbsp (24 g) all-purpose flour

2 cups (480 ml) nondairy milk

½ cup (57 g) vegan Cheddar-style shreds

½ cup (56 g) vegan mozzarella-style shreds

4 medium Yukon gold potatoes, sliced very thin

In a large nonstick skillet over medium-high heat, heat the olive oil. Add the onion and sauté, reducing the heat as needed, until it starts to brown, about 10 minutes. Drizzle the agave over the onion, and season with a pinch of salt and pepper. Toss and continue to sauté until the onion is golden brown, another 15 to 20 minutes.

Preheat the oven to 400°F (204°C).

When the onion is golden brown, add the butter to the skillet. Once the butter is melted, add the flour, and whisk to combine.

Pour the milk into the skillet, and whisk to combine, making sure there are no lumps of flour left in the sauce. Season with a pinch of salt and pepper. Bring to a simmer, reduce the heat to medium-low, and simmer until the sauce has thickened, 2 to 3 minutes. Add the Cheddar and mozzarella to the skillet, and whisk to combine. Continue whisking until the cheeses have melted into the sauce. Taste and adjust seasoning.

Pour about a third of the sauce with the onion into a 9 x 13–inch (23 x 33–cm) baking dish. Layer half of the thinly sliced potatoes on top of the sauce in the baking dish. Sprinkle the potatoes with a few pinches of salt and pepper. Then pour a third more of the sauce over the potatoes. Layer the remaining potatoes, and sprinkle the top of those potatoes with a few pinches of salt and pepper. Pour the remaining sauce over the top of the potatoes.

Cover the baking dish with aluminum foil, and bake for 60 to 75 minutes, or until the potatoes are tender. Let them sit for 5 to 10 minutes, then serve.

*See photo on page 105.

Garlic Alfredo Spaghetti Squash

We all know spaghetti squash is a more nutritious alternative to pasta, but this recipe has all the most important traits that you want in a delicious Alfredo pasta: it's savory, cheesy, carby, filling and seriously comforting. You can't go wrong with serving this dish at your festive gathering. And because it's healthier than regular pasta, your guests won't feel bad for going back for seconds, thirds or tenths or whatever. I don't judge.

Serves 4

1 medium spaghetti squash

2 tbsp (30 ml) extra-virgin olive oil

Salt and pepper, to taste

2 tbsp (28 g) vegan butter

2 shallots, diced

6 cloves garlic, finely chopped

2 tbsp (16 g) all-purpose flour

2 cups (480 ml) nondairy milk

½ tsp lemon zest (optional)

1 tbsp (15 ml) lemon juice

½ cup (50 g) vegan Parmesan

½ cup (56 g) vegan mozzarella

Preheat the oven to 400°F (204°C).

Cut the spaghetti squash in half lengthwise. Rub the inside and outside of each half with the olive oil, and sprinkle with a pinch of salt and pepper. Place, cut side down, on a large baking sheet. Roast for 30 to 40 minutes, or until the inside of the squash is fork-tender.

When the squash is almost done roasting, make the Alfredo sauce. In a large nonstick skillet over medium-high heat, heat the butter. Once the butter is melted, add the shallots and garlic. Sauté, reducing the heat as needed, for 1 to 2 minutes, or until the shallots are translucent.

Add the flour, and whisk to combine, making a roux. It should look like a paste. Let it simmer for 1 minute. Pour in the milk, and whisk to combine, making sure there are no lumps. Season with a few pinches of salt and pepper. Bring the mixture to a simmer, and whisk frequently, letting the sauce thicken, 2 to 3 minutes.

Add the lemon zest, if using, lemon juice and the Parmesan. Whisk to combine. Let the sauce simmer for another minute to let the Parmesan melt into the sauce. Taste and adjust seasonings, adding more salt or pepper if needed. Reduce the heat to low.

Once the squash is done, scrape the seeds out of the center and discard them. Using a fork, scrape the inside of each squash and create the squash ribbons that look like spaghetti. Scrape as much of the inside of each squash out of the center as you can, and add it to the skillet with the Alfredo sauce.

Toss all the spaghetti squash with the Alfredo sauce, then fill the insides of each squash back up with the mixture. Top the filling with the mozzarella, and bake for 10 minutes to melt the cheese as much as possible. If you want to brown them slightly, broil for 1 to 2 minutes.

Serve immediately.

Crispy Herbed Sweet Potato Stacks

Once, at a fancy New York City restaurant, I ordered something fairly unassuming—but it was quite literally life-changing. It was a tiny, crispy potato stack and it had no business being that delicious. In honor of that stack, I give you a stack of your very own. If you're cooking for a special event and don't want to go the scalloped potatoes route, this is an excellent alternative. These sweet potato stacks are so buttery and full of flavor. Cut into one, and see savory clumps of garlic and herbs. Literal layers of sweet potato goodness.

Serves 4

3 medium sweet potatoes

¼ cup (54 g) vegan butter, melted

¼ cup (60 ml) extra-virgin olive oil

1 tbsp (2 g) fresh thyme leaves

1 tbsp (2 g) fresh rosemary, chopped

1 tbsp (4 g) fresh sage, chopped

4 cloves garlic, finely chopped

Pinch of ground cinnamon

A few pinches of salt and pepper

Preheat the oven to 400°F (204°C). Spray a 12-cup muffin tin with nonstick spray.

Using a mandoline or a knife, cut the sweet potatoes into very thin rounds. You don't want them to be translucent, but almost that thin. Set aside.

In a medium mixing bowl, combine the butter, olive oil, thyme, rosemary, sage, garlic, cinnamon and a few pinches of salt and pepper. Whisk to combine. Add the sliced sweet potatoes to the bowl, and toss to coat all of the slices evenly.

Layer the sweet potatoes one slice on top of the other in one of the muffin cups until you fill the cup up. Repeat with all the sweet potatoes. You should be able to fill all 12 cups. Sprinkle the tops of the sweet potato stacks with a little bit of salt.

Cover the pan with aluminum foil, and bake, covered, for 30 minutes. Uncover and bake for another 20 to 25 minutes, or until the outsides of the sweet potato stacks are brown and crispy.

*See photo on page 108.

Stir-Fried Ginger-Sesame Green Beans

So you've been chosen (or signed up) to bring the green bean dish to the holiday get together. You *could* bring the normal and underwhelming green bean casserole that everyone just expects to be there, *or* you could jazz up the dinner table and delightfully surprise everyone with these Asian-inspired green beans. This recipe has an amazing flavor with the perfect amount of "kick." Don't be surprised if people ask you for the recipe at the end of the night.

Serves 4

1 lb (454 g) green beans, trimmed

3 tbsp (45 ml) sesame oil, divided

1 tbsp (15 ml) soy sauce

1 tbsp (15 ml) rice wine vinegar

2 tbsp (30 ml) sweet soy sauce

6 cloves garlic, finely chopped

1 tbsp (6 g) fresh ginger, grated

Pinch of red pepper flakes

1 tbsp (9 g) sesame seeds

Chili oil (page 94), for topping (optional)

Blanch the green beans. Bring a large pot of salted water to a boil. Prepare an ice bath: fill a large bowl with cold water and ice.

Add the green beans to the pot, and boil for 1 minute, then transfer the green beans to the ice bath. Let them cool for about 5 minutes.

In a small mixing bowl, whisk together 1 tablespoon (15 ml) of the sesame oil, the soy sauce, rice wine vinegar, sweet soy sauce, garlic, ginger and red pepper flakes.

In a large nonstick skillet over medium-high heat, heat the remaining 2 tablespoons (30 ml) of sesame oil. Drain the green beans, and add them to the skillet. Sauté, reducing the heat as needed, until the beans begin to brown and soften, 5 to 7 minutes. Pour the sauce over the green beans, and continue to sauté until the green beans are very soft, 3 to 5 minutes.

Sprinkle the green beans with the sesame seeds and toss to combine. Serve immediately with chili oil, if desired.

*See photo on page 108.

Garlicky Harissa Roasted Carrots

I know your first thought probably isn't to make harissa for roasted carrots. Growing up spending holidays in the South with my grandma's family from Kentucky, the carrot dishes were sweet ones: maple roasted and sugary. Well, everything was sugary. However, when I tell you this spicy harissa was made for these garlicky roasted carrots, I really mean it. It is an actual celestial experience to eat these beautiful carrots. Top them with some pistachios and pomegranate seeds. A crumble of vegan cheese perhaps. This is where it's at.

Serves 4

Carrots
1 lb (454 g) carrots, peeled, thick ones sliced in half lengthwise

2 tbsp (30 ml) extra-virgin olive oil

10 cloves garlic, finely chopped

Pinch of salt and pepper

Harissa
10 dried chilies, a combination of mild and spicy (guajillo, de arbol and chipotle)

6 oz (170 g) roasted red peppers

2 tbsp (32 g) tomato paste

2 tbsp (30 ml) lemon juice

1 tbsp (15 ml) apple cider vinegar

6 cloves garlic

1 tsp ground caraway seeds

2 tsp (3 g) coriander

1 tsp cumin

1 tsp smoked paprika

Pinch of cayenne

Pinch of salt and pepper

1 slice vegan crusty bread

¼ cup (60 ml) extra-virgin olive oil, plus more as needed

For Serving (Optional)
Pistachios, chopped

Pomegranate seeds

Vegan soft cheese

Preheat the oven to 400°F (204°C).

Make the carrots. Place the carrots in a large mixing bowl. Pour the olive oil over the carrots, then add the garlic and salt and pepper. Toss to combine everything.

Pour the carrots, garlic and oil out onto a baking sheet. Spread the carrots out evenly, and roast for 15 to 17 minutes, or until they are tender and starting to brown.

While the carrots roast, make the harissa. Put the dried chilies in a large mixing bowl, then pour warm water over the chilies until they are fully covered. Let them sit for 5 to 10 minutes, or until they have softened. Drain and remove the seeds from the chilies as much as you can.

Meanwhile, in a food processor, combine the roasted red peppers, tomato paste, lemon juice, apple cider vinegar, garlic, caraway seeds, coriander, cumin, smoked paprika, cayenne and a pinch of salt and pepper. Break the slice of bread up into pieces, and add to the food processor.

When the dried chilies are soft, add them to the food processor as well. Start processing the mixture, and stream in the olive oil. Continue to process until the mixture is completely smooth, 2 to 3 minutes.

Serve the roasted carrots with the harissa on top. Sprinkle with pistachios, pomegranate seeds and soft cheese, if desired.

Salted Sweet Butter Parker House Rolls

Everyone loves a good roll. However, we all know that not all rolls are created equal. These are the cream of the crop. While bread rolls are usually a supporting act for the main dish, these rolls are a standout star all on their own. They also make the perfect dipping bread for those mashed potatoes. This recipe makes twelve, so you'll have plenty to save for yourself and *maybe* share with others.

Yields 12 rolls

1 cup (240 ml) warm oat milk (about 110°F [43°C])

2½ tsp (8 g) active dry yeast

3 tbsp (39 g) organic cane sugar

3 cups (375 g) all-purpose flour, plus more for dusting

¼ cup (48 g) potato starch

1½ tsp (9 g) salt

¼ cup (54 g) vegan butter, melted and cooled slightly

¼ cup (60 ml) applesauce

Topping
⅓ cup (72 g) vegan butter, melted

1 tbsp (15 ml) agave syrup

Sea salt

Make the rolls. In the bowl of a stand mixer, combine the oat milk, yeast and sugar. Stir and let sit for about 5 minutes, until the mixture gets bubbly and frothy.

In a separate mixing bowl, sift together the flour and potato starch, then stir in the salt. Set aside.

Add the melted butter and applesauce to the bowl of the stand mixer, and mix using the dough hook. While the dough hook is running, begin adding the dry ingredients about ½ cup (60 g) at time, until all of the dry ingredients are incorporated.

Once the dough comes together and forms a ball, let the dough hook knead the dough for about 2 minutes. If the dough is still sticky, add another tablespoon (8 g) of flour at a time until the dough is no longer sticky. Put the dough in a large bowl that has been sprayed with nonstick spray. Cover and put in a warm dry, place. Let rise for about an hour or until the dough has doubled in size.

Punch down the dough, then turn the dough out onto a floured surface. Roll the dough out into a rectangle that is about ½ inch (1.3 cm) thick. Divide the dough into twelve equal squares. Take one square, and fold one side of the dough over the other, so there is a fold in the center. Repeat with all of the squares.

Spray the bottom of a large baking dish with nonstick spray. Then place all of the rolls in the baking dish right up against each other. Cover the dish, and let the rolls rise for 45 minutes, or until doubled in size.

Preheat the oven to 350°F (176°C).

Make the topping. Whisk together the butter and agave, and brush the tops of the rolls with about half of the mixture.

Bake for 20 to 25 minutes, or until the rolls are firm and golden brown. Brush the tops of the rolls with the remaining butter mixture, and sprinkle with sea salt. Let the rolls cool slightly, break them apart and serve.

*See photo on page 113.

"Bacon"-Wrapped Dates

There is something drool-inducing, daydream-creating and honestly completely distracting about these dates. The combination of sweet, chewy dates and salty, creamy cheese, plus the crispy, herby, smoky "bacon" is unlike anything else. These dates are something I am constantly throwing together for parties. They are the easiest finger food on the planet, so festive, and they will get rave reviews. People won't stop talking about them, so get ready to feel pretty dang good about yourself.

Yields 16 dates

10 oz (283 g) Medjool dates, pitted (about 16 dates)

4 oz (113 g) soft vegan cheese (feta, fresh mozzarella, nut cheese, etc.)

16 slices vegan bacon

¼ cup (60 ml) extra-virgin olive oil

1 tbsp (15 ml) agave syrup

2 tsp (1 g) fresh thyme leaves or rosemary, chopped

Preheat the oven to 400°F (204°C).

Slice each date lengthwise, being careful to only slice one side and not all the way through the date. You just want to create a pocket. Fill the date pockets with about 1 teaspoon of the cheese. Smush the date back together around the vegan cheese. Wrap a slice of bacon around the date. Secure with one or two toothpicks. Repeat with all of the dates, placing them on a baking sheet.

In a small mixing bowl, whisk together the olive oil and agave. Add the thyme and whisk again. Brush the outside of each of the wrapped dates with the olive oil mixture.

Bake the dates for 10 to 15 minutes, or until the bacon is brown and a little crunchy.

Serve immediately.

*See photo on page 113.

Playful
PARTY FOODS

Parties and hangouts are obviously a good time, but the best part of a party is the food. Finger foods, themed foods and celebratory foods just make people happy.

The recipes in this chapter were created to incite joy and nostalgia at your fun and casual get together. They are all plant-based but full of the fun everyone wants and looks forward to at a party. The Buffalo Chick'n Spring Rolls (page 122) will disappear so fast, make sure you eat one before they're gone. The Taco Fries with Cheezy Chorizo Dip (page 119) are mouth-wateringly delicious. The Baby Fried Onions (page 127) . . . I mean who wouldn't love a mini fried onion?

Bring any of the recipes in this chapter to your Fourth of July cookout, potluck, Super Bowl party or birthday bash, and expect to see people just "hangin' out" at the end of the table where your food resides. Just make sure you get some, too.

Taco Fries with Cheezy Chorizo Dip

I'm confident you and your friends will enjoy this Mexican-inspired recipe featuring the most-loved form of potatoes. That's right. Taco fries and a ridiculously delicious cheezy chorizo dip. Years ago, I fell in love with a vegan chorizo queso fundido at a restaurant I frequented in Manhattan. I tried to re-create it here. Instead of tortilla chips, I made yummy taco fries with a homemade taco seasoning. However, feel free to use store-bought taco seasoning if you'd like.

Serves 4

Taco Fries
1 tsp chili powder

1 tsp salt

½ tsp cumin

½ tsp black pepper

½ tsp smoked paprika

½ tsp garlic powder

¼ tsp onion powder

¼ tsp Mexican oregano

Pinch of cayenne pepper

4 large Russet potatoes

2 tbsp (30 ml) extra-virgin olive oil

Cheezy Chorizo Dip
3 tbsp (42 g) vegan butter

8 oz (226 g) vegan chorizo sausage

3 cloves garlic, grated

1 cup (242 g) crushed tomatoes

⅓ cup (35 g) pickled jalapeños, diced

2 tbsp (16 g) all-purpose flour

1 cup (240 ml) nondairy milk

Salt and pepper, to taste

1 cup (113 g) vegan Cheddar-style shreds

⅓ cup (5 g) fresh cilantro, chopped, divided

Preheat the oven to 450°F (232°C).

Make the fries. In a small bowl, stir together the chili powder, salt, cumin, black pepper, paprika, garlic powder, onion powder, oregano and cayenne.

Wash and cut the potatoes into wedges. Put them in a large mixing bowl. Drizzle the olive oil over the potatoes, and toss to coat. Sprinkle the seasoning mixture over the potatoes, and toss to evenly coat.

Put the potato wedges in a single layer on a large baking sheet. Bake for 20 minutes, flip and bake for another 15 to 20 minutes, or until the potatoes are golden brown and completely cooked through.

While the potatoes bake, make the dip. In a large nonstick skillet over medium-high heat, heat the butter. Once the butter is melted, add the chorizo, and sauté, reducing the heat as needed, for 2 to 3 minutes, or until the chorizo is getting brown.

Add the garlic, crushed tomatoes and pickled jalapeños to the skillet, and toss to combine everything. Sauté for another 1 to 2 minutes.

Whisk the flour into the skillet, making sure it is fully combined. Pour in the milk and a few pinches of salt and pepper. Whisk again, making sure there are no lumps of flour left. Bring to a simmer, and let the sauce thicken for 2 to 3 minutes.

Stir in the Cheddar, and whisk frequently until it has melted completely. Taste and adjust seasonings, then add about ¼ cup (4 g) of the cilantro.

Once the fries are done, serve them immediately with the cheezy chorizo dip, topping the dip with the remaining cilantro.

Lenore's Everything Bagel Pretzel Bites with Chive Cream Cheeze Dip

Who doesn't love bite-sized versions of their favorite foods? And who doesn't love an everything bagel? Seriously. Give me names. I'll find them and convert them with these babies. These are named after my daughter because, well, she loves soft pretzels and would eat an everything bagel for breakfast every day for the rest of her life if she could. She also must have cream cheese for her bagels in the refrigerator at all times. When she tried these fresh right out of the oven, she asked if I could put them in her lunch box every day, and honestly, they are so easy that it wouldn't be difficult.

Serves 12

Pretzel Bites
1 lb (454 g) vegan pizza dough
All-purpose flour, for dusting
8 cups (1.9 L) water
⅓ cup (73 g) baking soda
¼ cup (60 ml) extra-virgin olive oil
3 tbsp (36 g) everything bagel seasoning

Chive Cream Cheeze Dip
8 oz (226 g) vegan cream cheese
⅓ cup (80 ml) nondairy milk or vegan whipping cream
2 cloves garlic, grated
½ tsp salt
Pinch of black pepper
¼ cup (12 g) fresh chives, chopped

Let the dough come to room temperature on the counter for 20 to 30 minutes.

Preheat the oven to 425°F (218°C). Line a baking sheet with parchment paper.

Make the pretzel bites. Put the dough on a floured surface. Roll the dough out into a rectangle that is about ½ inch (1.3 cm) thick. Cut the dough into 1 x 1–inch (2.5 x 2.5–cm) squares.

Bring the water to a boil in a large pot, then add the baking soda.

Put the dough squares into the boiling baking soda water, working in batches so you don't overcrowd the pot. Boil them for about 45 seconds, then remove them from the water and place them on the prepared baking sheet. Repeat with all the dough, boiling and placing each square on the baking sheet. Place them just a little bit apart from each other; they will puff up slightly.

Brush the tops of each square with the olive oil, then sprinkle each with a little bit of the everything bagel seasoning, making sure it sticks to the top. Bake for 15 to 20 minutes, or until the pretzel bites are golden brown.

While the pretzel bites bake, make the dip. In a large mixing bowl or the bowl of a stand mixer, combine the cream cheese and milk. Whip together. Add the garlic, salt and pepper. Continue to whip until everything is fully combined and the cream cheese is fluffy. Fold in the chives, then put the dip in the refrigerator until ready to serve.

Once the pretzel bites are done, serve them warm with the dip.

*See photo on page 118.

Jalapeño Popper Loaded Nachos

I absolutely love jalapeño poppers, and I adore nachos, but I am rarely able to eat them out at restaurants. There just aren't that many vegan nachos out there. So I made my own. The cheeze sauce is made with delicious vegan cream cheese and has jalapeños mixed in. After drizzling the cheeze sauce over your chips, top with vegan Cheddar, then the vegan bacon and then top with even more jalapeños. Now you've got yourself the best loaded nachos in the whole universe.

Serves 4

1 tbsp (15 ml) extra-virgin olive oil

6 cloves garlic, grated

1 cup (105 g) pickled jalapeños, divided

8 oz (226 g) vegan cream cheese

¾ cup (180 ml) nondairy milk

Salt and pepper, to taste

1 (9-oz [225-g]) bag tortilla chips

5 oz (142 g) vegan bacon, cooked and chopped

½ cup (57 g) vegan Cheddar-style shreds

Fresh jalapeños (optional)

Preheat the oven to 425°F (218°C).

In a large nonstick skillet over medium high heat, heat the olive oil. Add the garlic and ½ cup (52 g) of the pickled jalapeños, reserving the rest.

Reduce the heat to medium, and sauté the garlic and jalapeños for 1 to 2 minutes. Add the cream cheese, milk and a pinch of salt and pepper. Whisk until the cream cheese has completely melted and everything is fully combined. Let it simmer for 2 to 3 minutes so the sauce will thicken slightly. Taste and adjust seasonings.

Lay the tortilla chips out on a large baking sheet. Pour the cream cheese sauce evenly over all of the chips. Sprinkle the chopped bacon evenly over the chips, and then sprinkle the Cheddar out evenly over the chips. Sprinkle the remaining ½ cup (53 g) of pickled jalapeños over the top of the chips.

Bake for 5 minutes, or until the Cheddar has melted as much as it can. Top with fresh jalapeños if desired. Serve immediately.

*See photo on page 118.

Buffalo Chick'n Spring Rolls

There is something about buffalo sauce, I think we can all agree. It's just science. So . . . for science . . . I mixed together buffalo soy curls, vegan cream cheese and ranch seasoning. Then I rolled that into spring roll wrappers and baked them until golden. Then I dipped them into the best vegan ranch. I don't think there is a human among us who won't go gaga over them.

Serves 4

Spring Rolls

1½ cups (63 g) soy curls, soaked and drained

¼ cup (54 g) vegan butter

¼ cup (60 ml) hot sauce

6 oz (170 g) room-temperature vegan cream cheese

½ tsp garlic powder

2 tbsp (6 g) chopped fresh chives

1 tsp dried dill or 1 tbsp (3 g) fresh dill

1 tsp onion powder

Pinch of salt and pepper

8 to 10 vegan spring roll wrappers

Extra-virgin olive oil or vegetable oil, for brushing the spring rolls

Ranch Dip

¾ cup (180 ml) vegan mayonnaise

2 tbsp (30 ml) oat milk or other nondairy milk

¼ cup (12 g) fresh chives, chopped

2 tbsp (8 g) fresh parsley, chopped

1 tbsp (3 g) fresh dill

2 tsp (10 ml) lemon juice

1 tsp onion powder

½ tsp salt

¼ tsp black pepper

Preheat the oven to 425°F (218°C). Spray a large baking sheet with nonstick spray.

Make the spring rolls. Chop the soy curls into small pieces, and set aside.

In a large nonstick skillet over medium heat, heat the butter. Add the soy curls, and sauté, reducing the heat as needed, until the soy curls are golden brown, 10 to 12 minutes. Pour the hot sauce over the soy curls, and toss to coat. Reduce the heat to low, and simmer for about 1 minute. Let the soy curls cool for about 5 minutes.

While the soy curls cool, in a large mixing bowl or the bowl of a stand mixer, combine the cream cheese, garlic powder, chives, dill, onion powder, salt and pepper. Beat the mixture together with a hand mixer or the paddle attachment of the stand mixer until the cream cheese is smooth and everything is fully combined.

Add the cooled buffalo soy curls to the cream cheese mixture, and beat once more for just a few seconds to combine.

Take a spring roll wrapper, and lay it flat on a plate or cutting board. Lay it so it looks like a diamond. Place about 2 tablespoons (30 g) of the filling about 2 inches (5 cm) from the corner of the wrapper closest to you. Roll the corner over the filling once. Gently press down on each side of the filling. Fold both the left and right sides of the wrapper toward the middle. Rub a little bit of water with your finger along the edges of the wrapper, and roll the spring roll until it is tight and looks like a cigar. Press the edges to seal. Repeat with all the filling; you should get eight to ten spring rolls.

Lay the spring rolls seam side down on the prepared baking sheet. Brush the tops with oil. Bake for 10 minutes, flip, brush the other side of the spring rolls with oil and bake for 5 to 7 more minutes, or until they are golden brown and crispy.

While the spring rolls bake, make the ranch dip. In a food processor, combine the mayonnaise, milk, chives, parsley, dill, lemon juice, onion powder, salt and pepper. Pulse until everything is fully combined and the herbs have been chopped up and evenly distributed, 1 to 2 minutes.

Once the spring rolls are done, serve with the ranch for dipping. The spring rolls reheat well in the oven.

Crispy Gochujang Soy Curls with Kimchi Dip

Two words. *Kimchi. Dip.* Yes, I made it up, and I'll just say it. The moment I tasted it, I was like "Lauren, you freaking genius!" These crispy gochujang soy curls are truly remarkable just by themselves. Not a person alive has the willpower to turn down one of these yummy skewers. However, dipped in the kimchi dip, they are unrelentingly delicious. They make any gameday, shall we say, bearable. Forget the meat, and make these.

Serves 6

Soy Curls

8 oz (226 g) soy curls, soaked and drained

⅓ cup (43 g) cornstarch

1 tsp chili flakes

1 tsp salt

¼ cup plus 1 tbsp (75 ml) vegetable oil, divided

2 tbsp (32 g) gochujang paste

2 tbsp (30 ml) agave syrup

¼ cup (55 g) vegan light brown sugar

¼ cup (60 ml) soy sauce or tamari

4 cloves garlic, finely chopped

1 (1-inch [2.5-cm]) piece fresh ginger, peeled and grated

1 tbsp (15 ml) sesame oil

1 tsp sesame seeds

Kimchi Dip

4 oz (113 g) room-temperature vegan cream cheese

¼ cup (38 g) vegan kimchi

1 tbsp (15 ml) liquid from the kimchi

1 tsp rice wine vinegar

1 green onion, chopped

Pinch of salt and pepper

Make the soy curls. Add the soy curls to a large mixing bowl. Sprinkle the cornstarch, chili flakes and salt over the soy curls, and toss to coat.

In a large nonstick skillet over medium-high heat, heat the ¼ cup (60 ml) of oil. Add the soy curls, and sauté until they are golden brown and crispy, 10 to 12 minutes.

While the soy curls cook, make the sauce. In a medium mixing bowl, whisk together the remaining tablespoon (15 ml) of vegetable oil, the gochujang, agave, brown sugar, soy sauce, garlic, ginger, sesame oil and sesame seeds. Whisk until fully combined.

Once the soy curls are nice and brown, pour the sauce over them, and toss to coat. Simmer for 1 to 2 minutes. Turn off the heat.

Make the dip. In a food processor, combine the cream cheese, kimchi, liquid from the jar of kimchi, rice wine vinegar, green onion and a pinch of salt and pepper. Pulse, scraping down the sides as needed, until the dip is smooth and fully combined, 1 to 2 minutes.

Serve by threading soy curls onto wooden skewers for easier dipping, or serve as is and just dip by hand or with toothpicks.

*See photo on page 123.

Supreme Pizza Rolls

These pizza rolls are like a more sophisticated version of all my childhood pizza favorites. I lived off of Bagel Bites® and Totino's™ Pizza Rolls® from ages eight to twelve. My blood type could only be described as type P (for pizza). These fluffy, cheezy, savory rolls make me so happy. They taste just like something I would have popped in the toaster oven as a kid, in the very best way. You can use this basic recipe to make any kind of pizza rolls you want. If you were just a classic pepperoni kid, you can skip the rest and just make the delicious soy curl pepperoni.

Yields 10 rolls

1 cup (42 g) soy curls, soaked and drained

1 tbsp (15 ml) liquid aminos

1 tbsp (15 ml) apple cider vinegar

1 tsp maple syrup

¼ tsp liquid smoke

1 tsp smoked paprika

½ tsp fennel seeds

¼ tsp garlic powder

Pinch of cayenne pepper

2 tbsp (30 ml) extra-virgin olive oil

1 lb (454 g) vegan pizza dough

All-purpose flour, for dusting

½ cup (120 ml) pizza sauce, plus more for dipping

¼ cup (45 g) black olives, sliced

⅓ cup (49 g) bell peppers, chopped

¼ cup (40 g) red onion, diced

1¼ cups (170 g) vegan mozzarella-style shreds

Extra-virgin olive oil, for brushing

1 tsp dried oregano

1 tsp dried basil

Preheat the oven to 450°F (232°C). Brush the inside of a 9 x 13–inch (23 x 33–cm) baking dish with oil.

Make the soy curl pepperoni. Chop the soy curls into smaller chunks, and put them in a medium mixing bowl.

In a small mixing bowl, whisk together the liquid aminos, apple cider vinegar, maple syrup, liquid smoke, smoked paprika, fennel seeds, garlic powder and cayenne pepper. Pour the mixture over the soy curls, and toss to combine.

In a large nonstick skillet over medium-high heat, heat the olive oil. Add the soy curls and any extra seasoning that is left in the bowl. Sauté, reducing the heat as needed, until the soy curls are brown and crispy, 5 to 7 minutes. Remove from the heat.

Make the pizza rolls. Roll the pizza dough out on a floured surface into a large rectangle that is about ¼ inch (6 mm) thick. Spread the pizza sauce evenly onto the dough. Sprinkle the black olives, bell peppers, red onion and mozzarella evenly over the top of the dough. Sprinkle on the soy curl pepperoni.

Roll the dough up horizontally, into a spiral, like a cinnamon roll. Cut the roll into about 2-inch (5-cm) rolls. Place them in the prepared baking dish. Brush the tops of the rolls with a little more olive oil, and sprinkle with the dried oregano and dried basil.

Bake the rolls for 15 to 20 minutes, or until the insides are cooked through and the outsides are golden brown. Serve with extra pizza sauce for dipping.

*See photo on page 123.

Baby Fried Onions

If you're a bloomin' onion fan, these cute little babies are for you. While they don't "bloom" like a typical bloomin' onion, the fried pearl onions are poppable little versions that stay true to the flavor, including the tangy, tasty dipping sauce that goes with them. Take these to your next get together and get used to hearing "These taste just like a bloomin' onion!" Yes, Sharon, they sure do. You're welcome.

Serves 4

Onions
16 oz (454 g) pearl onions
1 cup (240 ml) nondairy milk
1 tsp apple cider vinegar
1 cup (125 g) all-purpose flour
1 tsp salt, plus more to taste
1 tsp garlic powder
1 tsp smoked paprika
½ tsp onion powder
½ tsp black pepper
Vegetable oil, for frying

Sauce
¼ cup (60 ml) vegan mayonnaise
1½ tbsp (23 ml) ketchup
1 tbsp (15 g) prepared horseradish
½ tsp soy sauce
Pinch of paprika
Pinch of cayenne pepper
Salt and pepper, to taste

Make the onions. Cut a cross into the top of each pearl onion, just to open them up slightly. Set aside.

In a medium mixing bowl, whisk together the milk and apple cider vinegar.

In a separate medium mixing bowl, whisk together the flour, salt, garlic powder, smoked paprika, onion powder and black pepper.

Put the pearl onions in the milk mixture, then put them into the flour mixture, then back in the milk mixture, and finally back into the flour mixture. Repeat with all of the pearl onions, making sure they all have a nice coating.

In a medium saucepan over medium-high heat, heat 2 to 3 inches (5 to 8 cm) of vegetable oil, enough to submerge the pearl onions in the oil. The oil will form tiny bubbles once it is hot enough.

Working in batches so you don't overcrowd the saucepan, fry the pearl onions, reducing the heat as needed, for 5 to 6 minutes, or until golden brown. Transfer the onions to a paper towel, and sprinkle them with a little more salt.

Make the sauce. In a small mixing bowl, whisk together the mayonnaise, ketchup, horseradish, soy sauce, paprika, cayenne and a pinch of salt and pepper. Taste and adjust seasonings.

Serve the onions with the sauce for dipping.

French Onion Potato Skins

These are the crispiest, crunchiest potato skins ever. They're perhaps only made better by the addition of the easiest and most incredible caramelized onion filling. The onions are cooked down until they melt in your mouth, plus they are simmered with some fresh thyme to give them even more of a French onion soup flavor. These are like little handheld cheesy soups, with potatoes replacing the traditional French bread topper.

Yields 12 potato skins

6 small to medium Russet potatoes

2 tbsp (28 g) vegan butter

2 large sweet onions, thinly sliced

Salt and pepper, to taste

2 tsp (10 ml) agave syrup

½ cup (120 ml) vegetable broth

2 sprigs fresh thyme

2 tbsp (30 ml) extra-virgin olive oil

1 cup (112 g) vegan mozzarella or Parmesan

Preheat the oven to 400°F (204°C).

Wash the potatoes, and poke holes all over the skin of each potato with a fork. Place the potatoes directly on the oven rack, and bake for 50 to 60 minutes, or until the potatoes are tender.

While the potatoes bake, make the caramelized onions. In a large nonstick skillet over medium-high heat, heat the butter. Add the onions, and sauté, reducing the heat to medium, until they start to become golden brown, about 30 minutes. Sprinkle with a pinch of salt and pepper, and drizzle the agave over the onions.

Continue to sauté until the onions are a deep golden brown, another 10 to 15 minutes. Pour in the vegetable broth, and add the thyme sprigs. Simmer the onions in the broth until it has all been absorbed, about 10 minutes. Remove the thyme sprigs from the skillet. Turn off the heat, and let the onions sit on the stove until you're ready to fill the potatoes.

Once the potatoes are tender, remove them from the oven, and let them cool. Increase the oven temperature to 450°F (232°C).

Once the potatoes are cool enough to handle, put a potato on its side, and slice completely through the center, creating two equal halves of potato. Repeat with all the potatoes, then scoop just the center of the potatoes out, leaving a little bit of the inside of the potato near the skin.

Place each potato half on a baking sheet. Brush the inside and the outside of each potato with the olive oil, and then sprinkle them with salt and pepper. Bake the potato skins for 10 minutes, flip them and bake for another 10 minutes.

Take the potato skins out of the oven, and fill each potato skin with 1 to 2 tablespoons (4 to 6 g) of the caramelized onions. Top each potato skin with some cheese, then broil on high for 2 to 4 minutes.

Serve immediately.

*See photo on page 126.

Pretzel Pigs in a Blanket with "Honey" Mustard

I have one question: What could possibly be better than a tiny vegan sausage, wrapped in a pretzel, and then dipped in "honey" mustard? Answer: Nothing. If you have friends coming over and need some finger foods, this is your sign to get your favorite vegan sausages. I like to use breakfast links, wrap them in some dough, and pretzel-fy them. You can pretty much pretzel-fy anything, and this is a very good use of that power.

Yields 12 to 14 pigs in a blanket

Pretzel Pigs in a Blanket
12 to 14 mini vegan sausages (I prefer breakfast links)

1 lb (454 g) vegan pizza dough

All-purpose flour, for dusting

8 cups (1.9 L) water

⅓ cup (73 g) baking soda

⅓ cup (72 g) vegan butter, melted

Sea salt, for topping

"Honey" Mustard
¼ cup (60 ml) vegan mayonnaise

¼ cup (60 ml) Dijon mustard

¼ cup (60 ml) agave syrup

Pinch of black pepper

Make the pigs in a blanket. Let the sausages thaw if they are frozen, and let the pizza dough come to room temperature on the counter.

Preheat the oven to 425° (218°C). Line a baking sheet with parchment paper.

Roll the pizza dough out on a floured surface to about ¼ inch (6 mm) thick. Cut strips of the pizza dough that are about 1 inch (2.5 cm) wide and 4 inches (10 cm) long. Make sure to cut as many strips as you have sausages. Wrap the dough strips around each sausage. Press the end of the dough down to seal.

Bring the water to a boil in a large pot, then add the baking soda. Working in batches, boil a few of the sausages wrapped in dough for about 45 seconds, then transfer them to the prepared baking sheet. Repeat with all the sausages.

Arrange the sausages about ½ inch (1.3 cm) apart on the baking sheet. Brush the tops with the melted butter, and sprinkle with salt. Bake for 15 to 20 minutes, or until golden brown.

While the sausages bake, make the "honey" mustard. In a small mixing bowl, whisk together the mayonnaise, Dijon, agave and pepper. Put the sauce in the refrigerator until ready to use.

When the pretzel pigs in a blanket are done, serve them warm with the "honey" mustard.

*See photo on page 126.

Al Pastor Loaded Fries

I don't have a regular cooking schedule, like other people. My job as a food blogger often requires me to make a dinner recipe at 8 a.m. or a dessert recipe at 5 a.m., depending on my posting schedule. So, I spend a lot of time eating dinner for breakfast and breakfast for dinner. I made a huge platter of these loaded fries at 9 a.m. so I could get the perfect photo. I told myself I would try and save some and eat them for dinner, but the platter was gone by about 10 a.m. They are so good. I couldn't stop myself. The spicy, crunchy tofu; the spicy adobo cheeze sauce; the sweet pineapple; the crispy fries; the toppings, oh lord, the toppings. They are addictive. You've been warned.

Serves 4

Al Pastor Tofu

1 cup (240 ml) vegetable broth

1 tbsp (15 ml) extra-virgin olive oil

1 tbsp (15 ml) apple cider vinegar

1 tsp Mexican dried oregano

1 tsp cumin

1 tsp salt

½ tsp ancho chile powder

1 chipotle pepper, finely chopped

1 tsp adobo sauce, from the can of chipotles

4 cloves garlic, finely chopped

1 (15-oz [425-g]) block extra-firm tofu, drained and pressed

Adobo Cheeze Sauce

2 tbsp (28 g) vegan butter

1 to 2 tsp (5 to 10 ml) adobo sauce

2 tbsp (16 g) all-purpose flour

1½ cups (360 ml) nondairy milk

Salt and pepper, to taste

1½ cups (170 g) Vegan Cheddar-style shreds

Make the tofu. In a large mixing bowl, whisk together the vegetable broth, olive oil, apple cider vinegar, oregano, cumin, salt, chile powder, chipotle pepper, adobo sauce and garlic.

Break up the block of tofu into small chunks, just with your fingers, and put it into the marinade. Toss to combine, and press the tofu down into the marinade as much as possible. Let the tofu marinate for at least an hour; you can do this ahead of time and leave the tofu in the marinade for as long as you want.

When you are ready to make the fries, preheat the oven to 450°F (232°C).

Pour the tofu, marinade and all, onto a large baking sheet. Spread the tofu out evenly. There will be liquid at the bottom of the pan; that's what you want. Bake for 20 minutes, toss the tofu and spread it back out. Bake for another 15 minutes, or until the tofu is golden brown and firm.

Meanwhile, make the cheeze sauce. In a large nonstick skillet over medium heat, heat the butter. Once the butter is melted, add the adobo sauce, using 1 teaspoon (5 ml) if you want it a little less spicy and 2 teaspoons (10 ml) if you want it a little spicier. Whisk to combine. Add the flour, and whisk to combine and make a roux. Let it simmer for about 1 minute.

Pour in the milk and a few pinches of salt and pepper. Whisk to combine, making sure there are no lumps of roux. Bring to a simmer, reduce the heat to medium-low, and let it simmer until the sauce thickens, 2 to 3 minutes.

Add the Cheddar, and whisk frequently until the cheese melts into the sauce. Taste and adjust seasonings. Reduce the heat to low, and keep warm until you're ready to put together the fries.

(continued)

Fries

1 (1-lb [454-g]) package frozen French fries, cooked according to package directions (see Note)

1 (8-oz [227-g]) can crushed pineapple, drained

Guacamole, vegan sour cream, salsa and fresh cilantro, for topping

Make the fries. When you are ready to put together the fries, put the cooked fries on a large platter. Layer about half the tofu, then half the cheeze sauce, then the rest of the tofu, the rest of the cheeze sauce, then the crushed pineapple. Top with guacamole, vegan sour cream, salsa and cilantro. Serve immediately.

Note: You can also cook the French fries in an air fryer.

Fried Green Chile Mac and Cheeze Dippers

I have been so intrigued and, dare I say, haunted by the idea of fried macaroni and cheese balls for a while. I feel like that has become a pretty popular appetizer that I have seen at a lot of restaurants, but I haven't been able to try them anywhere. So, I wanted to make us all a very tasty option that will make everyone else jealous. These were a bit of trial and error. Dairy-free cheese doesn't firm up like regular cheese, so I had to figure out how to bind the balls together. I think my hard work will serve you well, because these are the bomb.

Serves 12

8 oz (226 g) macaroni

2 tbsp (28 g) vegan butter

1 (4-oz [113-g]) can green chiles

2 tbsp (16 g) all-purpose flour

1½ cups (360 ml) oat milk or other nondairy milk

Salt and pepper, to taste

1 cup (113 g) vegan Cheddar-style shreds

2 cups (112 g) panko breadcrumbs, divided

½ cup (120 ml) vegan egg

Vegetable oil, for frying

Vegan ranch or barbecue sauce, for dipping

Make the macaroni. Cook the macaroni according to package directions, and drain when it is al dente. I like to toss the macaroni with a drizzle of olive oil so it doesn't stick together.

Make the cheeze sauce. In a large pot over medium heat, heat the butter. Once the butter is melted, add the green chiles, and sauté for about a minute. Pour in the flour, and whisk to combine and create a roux. Let it simmer for a minute.

Pour in the milk and a few pinches of salt and pepper, then whisk to fully combine and make sure there are no lumps of roux left. The only lumps should be the chiles. Let the milk come to a simmer, reduce the heat to medium-low, and let it simmer until it thickens, 2 to 3 minutes. Add the Cheddar to the pot, and whisk frequently until the cheese melts into the sauce. Taste and adjust seasonings.

Pour the cooked macaroni into the pot with the cheeze sauce, and toss to combine. Let the macaroni and cheeze cool for 15 to 20 minutes on the stove. Place it in the refrigerator to cool completely, 3 to 4 hours.

Once the macaroni and cheeze has cooled, add ⅔ cup (37 g) of the panko breadcrumbs to the pot with the macaroni and cheeze, as well as the egg. These will help to bind it. Stir until everything is fully incorporated.

Put the remaining 1⅓ cups (75 g) of panko breadcrumbs into a bowl. Take small scoops of the mixture (I like to use a tiny cookie or ice cream scoop), and roll the scoop into a ball. Put the ball into the panko breadcrumbs, and coat the entire outside. Repeat with all the macaroni and cheeze mixture.

In a medium saucepan over medium-high heat, heat 2 to 3 inches (5 to 8 cm) of vegetable oil, enough to submerge the macaroni balls in it. Working in batches, fry the macaroni and cheeze balls for 2 to 3 minutes, or until they are golden brown and crunchy.

Serve immediately with ranch or barbecue sauce.

*See photo on page 131.

Hearty
VEGGIE-CENTRIC DISHES

Non-vegans sometimes have a hard time perceiving vegetable-focused dishes as hearty or substantial, but that's exactly what the recipes in this next chapter are. They all check the boxes of satisfying, filling and obviously delicious.

These dishes feature more than just veggies, however. You can expect that, in this chapter, yummy vegetables are the heroines and leading roles in these recipes. Crispy Orange-Sesame Brussels Sprouts and Rice (page 137) are so, so good, you'll keep coming back for more. The Potato and "Chorizo" Tacos (page 140) are a fun take on a classic taco but even more filling and crave-worthy. The Sweet Potato Gnocchi with Sage Butter (page 152) is a lighter take on the regular potato gnocchi. Its savory flavor paired with the earthy sage butter is just . . . *chef's kiss.*

Crispy Orange-Sesame Brussels Sprouts and Rice

This takeout-inspired dish is seriously delectable. A great alternative to orange chicken, these sprouts are perfectly crispy without being fried, and this sauce is so good I would name a child after it, or at least a dog or mouse or something. So, the next time you're tempted to click on that delivery app, try this instead. You will be happy you did.

Serves 4

Brussels Sprouts
Nonstick cooking spray

1¼ cups (300 ml) soy milk or other nondairy milk

1 tsp rice wine vinegar

¾ cup (94 g) all-purpose flour

½ cup (68 g) cornstarch

2 tsp (10 ml) soy sauce

2 cups (112 g) panko breadcrumbs

1 lb (454 g) Brussels sprouts, trimmed and halved or quartered

Sauce
1 cup (240 ml) orange juice

2 tbsp (16 g) cornstarch

⅓ cup (80 ml) vegetable broth

⅓ cup (80 ml) soy sauce

3 tbsp (45 ml) agave syrup

2 tsp (10 ml) rice wine vinegar

2 tsp (4 g) orange zest

6 cloves garlic, grated

2 tsp (4 g) fresh ginger, grated

2 tbsp (18 g) sesame seeds

3 to 4 dried Thai chilies (optional)

For Serving
2 cups (372 g) cooked jasmine or white rice

Green onions (optional)

Sesame seeds (optional)

Preheat the oven to 425°F (218°C). Line a baking sheet with parchment paper, and spray with nonstick spray.

Start the Brussels sprouts. In a small mixing bowl or liquid measuring cup, whisk together the milk and rice wine vinegar. Set aside for 2 to 3 minutes.

Gather two medium mixing bowls. In the first bowl, add the flour and cornstarch. Pour in the milk and vinegar mixture and the soy sauce. Whisk the wet ingredients into the dry ingredients until fully combined and you have a smooth batter. In the second bowl, add the panko breadcrumbs.

Dip each Brussels sprout into the wet batter, coating completely, then put them into the panko breadcrumbs and coat completely. Place them on the prepared baking sheet. Repeat with all of the Brussels sprouts.

Spray the tops of the Brussels sprouts with more nonstick spray. Bake for 15 minutes. Flip the Brussels sprouts with tongs, and bake for another 15 to 20 minutes, or until they are crispy on the outside and tender inside.

While the Brussels sprouts bake, make the sauce. In a medium saucepan, whisk together the orange juice and cornstarch, making sure there are no lumps of cornstarch left. Add the vegetable broth, soy sauce, agave, rice wine vinegar, orange zest, garlic and ginger. Whisk to combine.

Heat the saucepan over medium heat, bring to a simmer, then reduce the heat to medium-low and simmer, whisking frequently, until the sauce thickens, 2 to 3 minutes. Add the sesame seeds and Thai chilies, if using, and simmer for another minute. Reduce the heat to low, and keep warm until the Brussels sprouts are done.

Transfer the Brussels sprouts to a large bowl, pour the sauce over them, and gently toss to coat.

Serve the Brussels sprouts over the rice, and top with green onions and more sesame seeds, if desired.

Cheezy Roasted Corn Enchiladas

I *love* this recipe. These enchiladas have a flavor that's truly unique and delicious. If you wake up one day with a hankering for Tex-Mex food, this recipe really checks that box. It also feeds a crowd, so feel free to make this dish for a party and blow everyone away with your corn-roasting and enchilada-creating abilities.

Serves 6

4 ears corn

3 poblano peppers, halved and deseeded

10 cloves garlic

2 tbsp (30 ml) extra-virgin olive oil

Pinch of salt and pepper

1½ cups (170 g) vegan Cheddar-style shreds, divided

1 tsp paprika

¼ tsp cumin

¼ tsp dried Mexican oregano

¼ tsp coriander

¼ tsp chipotle powder

6 or 7 flour or corn tortillas

1 cup (240 ml) green or red enchilada sauce

Toppings of choice

Preheat the oven to 425°F (218°C).

Put the whole ears of corn, the halved poblanos and the garlic on a baking sheet. Drizzle the olive oil over the vegetables. Sprinkle with a pinch of salt and pepper, and toss to coat.

Roast for about 25 minutes, or until the poblanos are soft and the corn is starting to brown. Leave the oven on, but remove the corn, poblanos and garlic, and let them cool for a few minutes, until cool enough to handle.

Cut the corn kernels off the cob. Put the corn, poblanos and garlic into a food processor. Add ½ cup (56 g) of the cheese, the paprika, cumin, oregano, coriander and chipotle powder. Pulse the food processor until it comes together but there is still some texture to it. You want a finely chopped mixture, not a paste. Taste and adjust seasonings.

Fill the center of each tortilla with a few tablespoons (45 g) of the corn, poblano and garlic mixture. Then roll the tortilla up.

Put about ½ cup (120 ml) of the enchilada sauce in the bottom of a baking dish, and spread it out evenly. Lay all the rolled tortillas into the baking dish, seam side down. Pour the remaining enchilada sauce over the top of the enchiladas, and spread the sauce out evenly.

Sprinkle the remaining 1 cup (113 g) of cheese over the enchiladas. Bake for 15 to 17 minutes, or until the cheese has melted and the enchiladas are hot and bubbly.

Serve immediately with your favorite toppings.

Potato and "Chorizo" Tacos

Everyone loves tacos. It's true, look it up. But will every person on the planet love these Potato and "Chorizo" Tacos? I can almost guarantee it.

These tacos incorporate the "chorizo" deliciousness and carby goodness that we all want from time to time. Throw it all in a beloved taco and *bam*. And they only take about 30 minutes to prepare. Now, stop reading and make these tacos. You won't regret it.

Yields 12 tacos

4 medium Yukon gold potatoes, diced

¼ cup (60 ml) extra-virgin olive oil

6 cloves garlic, finely chopped

½ tsp salt

½ tsp paprika

¼ tsp chipotle powder

¼ tsp coriander

¼ tsp dried oregano

9 oz (255 g) vegan chorizo

12 soft or hard tortillas

Toppings of choice

In a large pot of room-temperature water, add the potatoes. Heat the pot over medium-high heat, and bring to a boil. Reduce the heat to a simmer, and simmer the potatoes for 15 to 20 minutes, or until they are fork-tender. Drain the potatoes.

In a large nonstick skillet over medium-high heat, heat the olive oil. Add the potatoes and the garlic to the skillet. Sprinkle the salt, paprika, chipotle, coriander and dried oregano over the potatoes and garlic. Toss to coat. Sauté, reducing the heat as needed, until the potatoes start to brown slightly, about 5 minutes.

Add the chorizo to the skillet, and toss to combine it with the potatoes. Continue to sauté for 2 to 3 minutes to heat the chorizo.

Using a potato masher or fork, mash the potatoes slightly, leaving lots of texture. Stir and sauté for another 1 to 2 minutes.

Turn off the heat, and fill your tortillas with a generous amount of the potato and "chorizo" mixture. Top with any toppings you want, and serve immediately.

*See photo on page 139.

Beer-Battered Mushroom Po' Boys with Horseradish Remoulade

New Orleans is one of my all-time favorite cities. Most people are inspired by the flavors and culture, and I am no different. Po' boys are simple and satisfying. I enjoyed a vegan po' boy while I was visiting the last time, and I decided that I wanted to put my own spin on this New Orleans staple. In place of the fried oysters, you'll find delicious beer-battered and fried shiitake mushrooms. Slather on some spicy horseradish remoulade, top with shredded lettuce and enjoy.

Serves 2

Horseradish Remoulade
¾ cup (180 ml) vegan mayonnaise

3 tbsp (45 ml) Dijon mustard

1½ tsp (4 g) paprika

1 tsp Cajun seasoning

1 tsp prepared horseradish

1 tsp pickle juice

½ to 1 tsp hot sauce

1 clove garlic, grated

Mushrooms
½ cup (120 ml) light beer

½ cup (120 ml) nondairy milk

2 tsp (10 ml) hot sauce

8 oz (226 g) shiitake mushrooms, halved or quartered

½ cup (63 g) all-purpose flour

½ cup (61 g) cornmeal

2 tsp (10 g) Cajun seasoning

½ tsp paprika

1 tsp salt, plus more to taste

½ tsp black pepper

Vegetable oil, for frying

Sandwiches
2 French baguettes or hoagie rolls

Shredded lettuce

Tomatoes, sliced

Make the horseradish remoulade. In a small mixing bowl, whisk together the mayonnaise, Dijon, paprika, Cajun seasoning, horseradish, pickle juice, hot sauce and garlic. Put the remoulade in the refrigerator until you're ready to make the sandwiches.

Make the mushrooms. In a medium mixing bowl, whisk together the beer, milk and hot sauce. Add the mushrooms to the bowl. Let the mushrooms sit in the liquid for about 15 minutes while you prepare the coating for the mushrooms.

In a separate medium mixing bowl, combine the flour, cornmeal, Cajun seasoning, paprika, salt and pepper.

When you are ready to fry the mushrooms, take the mushrooms out of the liquid, and put them into the bowl with the dry ingredients, tossing to coat the mushrooms completely.

In a large nonstick skillet, heat 1 to 2 inches (2.5 to 5 cm) of vegetable oil. A cast-iron skillet is preferable. The oil is ready when tiny bubbles are forming in the oil. Working in batches, fry the mushrooms for 2 to 3 minutes, or until they are golden brown.

Once the mushrooms are done, transfer them to a paper towel, and sprinkle with a little more salt.

Make the po' boys. Slice the baguettes or hoagie rolls in half, then spread the remoulade on the top and bottom. Put half the mushrooms into the roll, drizzle with a little more remoulade, and top with lettuce and tomato. Serve immediately.

*See photo on page 142.

Fried Pickle Sammies with Coleslaw

Who doesn't love a freakin' fried pickle chip? Since I have your attention, I'd like to declare that fried pickle chips are far superior to fried spears, and I'm prepared to die on that hill. The crunch to pickle ratio is absolutely perfect. Salty, crunchy, briny pickles and a creamy, slightly sweet coleslaw on some ciabatta bread will result in a flavor explosion in your mouth. I mean, c'mon, doesn't that sound amazing? It's simple and delicious.

Serves 4

Coleslaw
1½ cups (105 g) green cabbage, shredded

1 cup (75 g) purple cabbage, shredded

½ cup (55 g) carrot, shredded

¼ cup (60 ml) vegan mayonnaise

2 tsp (10 ml) apple cider vinegar

1 tsp organic cane sugar

½ tsp celery salt

Salt and pepper, to taste

Pickles
½ cup (63 g) all-purpose flour

1 tsp salt, plus more to taste

1 tsp paprika, plus more to taste

¼ tsp cayenne pepper

¼ tsp black pepper

½ cup (120 ml) nondairy milk

2 cups (286 g) dill pickles, sliced

Vegetable oil, for frying

Sandwiches
4 ciabatta rolls, sliced in half

Vegan mayonnaise

Make the coleslaw. In a medium mixing bowl, combine the shredded green and purple cabbage and the carrot.

In a small mixing bowl, whisk together the mayonnaise, apple cider vinegar, sugar, celery salt and a pinch of salt and pepper. Pour into the bowl with the cabbage and carrot. Toss to combine. Put the coleslaw in the refrigerator until ready to use.

Make the pickles. In a medium mixing bowl, whisk together the flour, salt, paprika, cayenne and black pepper. Pour the milk into the bowl, and whisk until smooth, making a wet batter for the pickles.

Put the pickle slices on a paper towel, and pat dry. Add about half the pickles to the batter, and coat completely. Leave them in the batter while you heat the oil.

In a large nonstick skillet over medium-high heat, heat 1 to 2 inches (2.5 to 5 cm) of vegetable oil. The oil is ready when tiny bubbles are forming in the oil. Scoop the pickles out of the batter with a slotted spoon, and let any excess batter drip off.

Put the pickles in the oil, and fry for 2 to 3 minutes, or until the pickles are golden brown. Transfer them to a paper towel when they are done, and sprinkle with a little more salt and paprika. Repeat with the rest of the pickles, putting them in the batter and then into the oil.

Once the pickles are done, make the sandwiches. Take a ciabatta roll, and spread the top and bottom with a little mayonnaise. Lay some of the fried pickles on the bottom of the roll, then top with some coleslaw. Repeat with remaining ingredients to make four sandwiches. Serve immediately.

*See photo on page 142.

Fried Green Tomato BLT

This BLT with fried green tomatoes is the *only* kind of BLT I enjoy. I just don't like tomatoes otherwise. The very first fried green tomato I ever tried was at a restaurant in Atlanta. It came with vegan bacon and crumbled cheeze on top—and a spicy sweet aioli. It was divine. It surprised me that I liked them since I hated all other tomatoes. I discovered that the "bacon" flavor *with* the cornmeal crust and the tart tomato was what did it for me. So I decided to turn this discovery into a sandwich by using the spicy-sweet aioli as the spread, fried green tomatoes, vegan bacon and butter lettuce. You're gonna love it.

Serves 4

Aioli
½ cup (120 ml) vegan mayonnaise

1 tbsp (15 ml) lemon juice

1 tsp Dijon mustard

½ tsp cayenne pepper

2 cloves garlic, grated

Pinch of salt

Fried Green Tomatoes
¾ cup (180 ml) soy milk or other nondairy milk

2 tbsp (16 g) cornstarch

1 cup (125 g) all-purpose flour

2 tsp (12 g) salt, divided

½ cup (61 g) cornmeal

½ cup (54 g) plain vegan breadcrumbs

½ tsp black pepper

½ tsp smoked paprika

4 green tomatoes, sliced about ½ inch (1.3 cm) thick

Vegetable oil, for frying

Sandwiches
8 slices vegan bread of choice

8 slices vegan bacon, cooked

Butter lettuce

Make the aioli. In a small mixing bowl, whisk together the mayonnaise, lemon juice, Dijon, cayenne, garlic and salt. Place the aioli in the refrigerator until you're ready to make the sandwiches.

Make the fried green tomatoes. In a medium mixing bowl, whisk together the milk and cornstarch.

Take two large plates, preferably with a large lip. On one plate, put the flour and ½ teaspoon of the salt. Stir to combine. On the second plate, combine the cornmeal, breadcrumbs, remaining 1½ teaspoons (9 g) of salt, black pepper and paprika. I like to use my fingers to mix together so the mixture doesn't go everywhere off the plate.

Take one slice of green tomato, dip it into the milk mixture, then put it on the plate with the flour and coat. Dip it back into the milk mixture, then put it on the plate with the cornmeal and breadcrumbs, and coat completely. Repeat with all of the tomato slices. Lay them on a plate.

In a large nonstick skillet over medium-high heat, heat about an inch (2.5 cm) of vegetable oil. A cast-iron skillet is preferable. The oil is ready when tiny bubbles are forming in it. Working in batches—about four slices at a time—fry the tomatoes, reducing the heat as needed, on one side for 2 to 3 minutes. Flip and fry for another 2 to 3 minutes, or until the tomato slices are golden brown. Place them on a paper towel when they are done. Repeat with the remaining tomatoes.

Make the BLTs. Spread some of the aioli on one slice of bread, lay two pieces of bacon on top, then a few fried green tomatoes. Drizzle a little more aioli onto the tomatoes, top them with butter lettuce, then spread a little more aioli on another slice of bread and put that on top. Repeat with the remaining ingredients.

Serve immediately.

*See photo on page 142.

Tangy Roasted Vegetable Panini with Lemon Aioli

This sandwich is crazy easy. You start by roasting some vegetables. You can use any vegetables you want. I used asparagus, mushrooms, Brussels sprouts and carrots, but feel free to switch it up. While the veggies roast and turn golden brown and juicy, make the lemon aioli. It's simple and tangy and goes shockingly well with the flavorful veggies. Slather aioli on both slices of bread, then add a generous helping of vegetables, a slice of your favorite vegan cheese, and then press. Don't worry if you don't have a panini press. You can lay something heavy to press—like cans of beans. Serve with chips, fries or a yummy pasta salad (I highly recommend the Dill Pickle Pasta Salad from my last cookbook, *Southern Vegan*).

Serves 2

Aioli
½ cup (120 ml) vegan mayonnaise

1 tsp lemon zest

2 tsp (10 ml) lemon juice

1 clove garlic, grated

Salt and pepper, to taste

Roasted Vegetables
4 cups vegetables, chopped (I like to use asparagus, mushrooms, carrots and Brussels sprouts)

3 tbsp (45 ml) extra-virgin olive oil

1 tbsp (15 ml) lemon juice

½ tsp lemon zest

½ tsp salt

¼ tsp black pepper

Paninis
4 slices crusty bread

2 slices vegan cheese

Preheat the oven to 375°F (190°C).

Make the aioli. In a small mixing bowl, whisk together the mayonnaise, lemon zest, lemon juice, garlic and a pinch of salt and pepper. Taste and adjust seasonings. Put the aioli in the refrigerator until you're ready to make the paninis.

Roast the vegetables. Put the chopped vegetables in a large mixing bowl, and drizzle the olive oil and lemon juice over the top. Toss to coat. Sprinkle the lemon zest, salt and pepper over the vegetables, and toss again.

Spread the vegetables out evenly on a large baking sheet with a rubber spatula. Roast for 15 minutes, toss the vegetables and roast for another 15 to 20 minutes, or until the vegetables are tender.

Make the paninis. Take one slice of the bread, spread with some of the aioli, then a slice of cheese. Top that with half the vegetables, then spread more aioli on another slice of bread. Put that on top of the vegetables. Repeat, making another panini.

Press the sandwiches, either using a panini press, or heat about 1 tablespoon (15 ml) of olive oil over medium-high in a large nonstick skillet. Put the sandwich in the skillet, and press with something heavy. I usually put a pizza pan on top and weigh it down with canned goods. Press for 2 to 3 minutes, then flip and press that side until the sandwich is golden brown on the outside.

Serve immediately.

*See photo on page 142.

Vietnamese-Inspired Sweet Potato Bowls

Bahn mi bowls, oh how I adore thee. These Vietnamese-inspired bowls feature the beloved pickled carrots, spicy mayonnaise and flavors that we all know and love in a traditional bahn mi sandwich. No surprise here, I've put my own little spin on this classic by making a comfy bowl version with fluffy rice and caramelized sweet potatoes as a replacement for the bread and meat protein. Filling, spicy and tangy, these flavor-packed rice bowls will be on regular rotation in your kitchen. You probably won't want to share.

Serves 4

Pickled Carrots
2 large carrots, julienned
¾ cup (180 ml) water
⅓ cup (80 ml) rice wine vinegar
¼ cup (51 g) organic cane sugar
2 tsp (12 g) salt

Sweet Potatoes
¼ cup (60 ml) sesame oil
2 cups (480 ml) vegetable broth
¼ cup (60 ml) soy sauce
2 tbsp (30 ml) rice wine vinegar
2 tbsp (28 g) vegan light brown sugar
4 cloves garlic, chopped
4 dried chiles, such as Thai or chile de arbol
4 medium sweet potatoes, sliced

Spicy Mayonnaise
½ cup (120 ml) vegan mayonnaise
2 tbsp (30 ml) sriracha

Bowls
1 cup (200 g) uncooked white rice
Sliced cucumbers
Chopped green onions
Chopped fresh cilantro

Make the pickled carrots. Add the carrots to a large heatproof bowl and set aside.

In a small saucepan, combine the water, rice wine vinegar, sugar and salt. Heat the saucepan over medium-high heat. Bring to a simmer, reduce the heat to low and simmer for 1 to 2 minutes, whisking periodically to make sure the sugar and salt have been absorbed. Remove from the heat, and pour the hot liquid over the carrots. Make sure they are all submerged, and let the carrots sit on the counter until everything else is ready.

Marinate the sweet potatoes. In a large mixing bowl, whisk together the sesame oil, vegetable broth, soy sauce, rice wine vinegar, brown sugar, garlic and chilies. Add the sliced sweet potatoes to the bowl, and make sure they are submerged. Let them marinate for at least an hour. You can marinate for an hour on the counter. If you plan to marinate longer, put the bowl in the refrigerator.

Once the sweet potatoes have marinated, preheat the oven to 400°F (204°C).

Remove the sweet potatoes from the marinade, and lay in a single layer on a large baking sheet. Pour about ½ cup (120 ml) of the marinade over the sweet potatoes. Bake for 15 minutes, flip the sweet potatoes over and bake for another 15 to 20 minutes, or until the sweet potatoes are soft and have browned a bit.

While the sweet potatoes bake, make the spicy mayonnaise. In a small mixing bowl, whisk together the mayonnaise and sriracha. Set aside.

Cook the rice according to package instructions.

When the sweet potatoes are done, assemble your bowls. Add some of the cooked rice to a bowl. Top with the sweet potatoes and pickled carrots, and drizzle with spicy mayonnaise. Top with cucumbers, green onions and cilantro, if desired. Serve immediately.

Hearty Green Goddess Roasted Veggie and Orzo Bowls

Stop! Don't skip over this recipe when you're thumbing through this book. These bowls are perfect for a weeknight meal. This recipe has "hearty" in the title because it truly is. It's an easy, tangy, comforting dish sure to please everyone seated at your table. You probably shouldn't plan on having leftovers, but do plan on keeping these ingredients on hand because it will most likely be requested again and again.

Serves 4

Green Goddess Dressing
1 cup (240 ml) vegan mayonnaise

1 cup (60 g) fresh parsley

¼ cup (13 g) fresh dill

¼ cup (4 g) fresh cilantro

¼ cup (23 g) fresh mint

¼ cup (12 g) fresh chives

½ tsp lemon zest

2 tbsp (30 ml) lemon juice

1 tbsp (15 ml) extra-virgin olive oil

1 tbsp (8 g) capers

2 cloves garlic

Pinch of salt and black pepper

Bowls
12 oz (340 g) asparagus, trimmed

1 lb (454 g) sweet peppers, halved

1 lb (454 g) baby potatoes, halved

¼ cup (60 ml) extra-virgin olive oil

1 tbsp (15 ml) lemon juice

4 cloves garlic, chopped

2 tbsp (6 g) fresh chives, chopped

2 tbsp (2 g) fresh cilantro, chopped

A few pinches of salt and pepper

16 oz (454 g) orzo, cooked

Make the green goddess dressing. In a food processor, combine the mayonnaise, parsley, dill, cilantro, mint, chives, lemon zest and juice, olive oil, capers, garlic and a pinch of salt and pepper. Blend, scraping down the sides as needed, until the sauce is smooth and the herbs are blended into the sauce, 1 to 2 minutes. Put the sauce in the refrigerator until you're ready to serve.

Preheat the oven to 400°F (204°C).

Make your vegetable bowl. In a large mixing bowl, combine the asparagus, peppers and baby potatoes. Drizzle with the olive oil and lemon juice. Add the garlic, chives and cilantro to the bowl, as well as a few pinches of salt and pepper. Toss the vegetables until fully coated in all the seasoning.

Spread the vegetables out onto a baking sheet, and roast for 25 to 30 minutes, or until the potatoes are soft and the asparagus and peppers are starting to brown.

Serve in a bowl with the cooked orzo in the bottom, the roasted vegetables on top, and drizzle the whole thing with the green goddess dressing.

*See photo on page 147.

Coconut Curry Cauliflower with Coconut Rice

I'm obsessed with curry, so I did a mildly crazy thing here. I merged two of my favorite types of curry and made a Thai- and Indian-inspired fusion. This is what culinary fantasies are made of.

Serves 4

Coconut Rice

1 (13.5-oz [399-ml]) can coconut milk

1 cup (240 ml) water

1 tbsp (13 g) cane sugar

½ tsp salt

2 cups (400 g) uncooked long-grain rice

Coconut Curry Cauliflower

3 tbsp (40 g) solid coconut oil

1 medium head cauliflower, cut into florets

1½ cups (165 g) snap peas or green beans

1 cup (149 g) mild peppers, sliced (such as bell peppers or shishito)

2 large carrots, sliced

Salt and red pepper flakes, to taste

¼ cup (60 ml) vegetable oil

1 (1-inch [2.5-cm]) piece fresh ginger, peeled and grated

10 cloves garlic, finely chopped

1 shallot, diced

1 tsp coriander seeds

2 tsp (4 g) curry powder

1 tsp garam masala

1 tsp turmeric

1 (15-oz [425-g]) can tomato sauce

1 (13.5-oz [399-ml]) can coconut cream or full-fat coconut milk

2 cups (480 ml) vegetable broth

2 tsp (10 ml) agave syrup, plus more to taste

2 tsp (10 ml) lemon juice, plus more to taste

For Serving

Toasted coconut

Fresh cilantro

Extra lemon

Make the coconut rice. In a medium saucepan, whisk together the coconut milk, water, sugar and salt. Stir in the rice. Heat the saucepan over medium-high heat, bring to a simmer, and stir one last time. Reduce the heat to low, and cover the saucepan. Simmer on low for 15 to 17 minutes. The liquid should be absorbed. Turn off the heat, and leave the saucepan covered to finish steaming for 10 more minutes, or until the rice is tender.

Meanwhile, make the coconut curry cauliflower. In a large pot or large sauté pan over medium-high heat, heat the coconut oil. Add the cauliflower, snap peas, peppers and carrots. Season with a pinch of salt and red pepper flakes. Sauté, reducing the heat as needed, for about 10 minutes. The cauliflower should begin to brown. Remove the vegetables from the pot or pan, put them in a large bowl and set aside.

In the same pot or pan, heat the vegetable oil over medium heat. Add the ginger, garlic and shallot. Sauté, reducing the heat as needed, for 1 to 2 minutes. Add in the coriander seeds, curry powder, garam masala and turmeric. Stir everything together, and sauté the spices for 1 to 2 minutes.

Pour in the tomato sauce, coconut cream, vegetable broth, agave, lemon juice, a few pinches of salt and a pinch of red pepper flakes. Whisk to combine. Bring to a simmer, reduce the heat to medium-low and add all the vegetables back into the pot or pan. Make sure the vegetables are as submerged as possible in the sauce. Simmer for about 15 minutes, or until the cauliflower is tender. Taste and adjust seasonings. It may need salt and some extra agave and lemon juice.

Serve the curry over the rice. I like to top it with toasted coconut, fresh cilantro and extra lemon.

*See photo on page 134.

Lillian's Lemon and Broccoli Flatbread

Julie's daughter, Lilly (and my daughter's best friend), is an old soul. She is a 10-year-old who loves all things fruit and veggie. No chocolate for Lilly; if it's healthy, she's into it. She does love some quintessential kid foods, though, so in her honor, I put together a sophisticated pizza. One that would satisfy her love of broccoli and also her love of cheesy goodness. This is kid- and adult-approved. Even Lilly's best friend, my daughter, Lenore, loves these flatbreads.

Serves 6

Flatbread Dough

2 cups (250 g) all-purpose flour, plus more for dusting

1 tsp baking powder

½ tsp baking soda

½ tsp salt

½ cup (120 ml) soy milk

½ cup (120 ml) vegan sour cream or plain yogurt

1 tsp agave syrup

Lemon-Garlic Oil

¼ cup (60 ml) extra-virgin olive oil

4 cloves garlic, grated

1 tbsp (6 g) lemon zest

Toppings

1 small head broccoli, cut into florets

1 tbsp (15 ml) extra-virgin olive oil

Salt and pepper, to taste

4 slices vegan bacon

2 cups (224 g) vegan mozzarella-style shreds

1 lemon, sliced very thinly

¼ cup (60 ml) agave syrup

½ tsp hot sauce

Make the flatbread dough. In a large mixing bowl, sift together the flour, baking powder and baking soda. Stir in the salt. Make a well in the center of the dry ingredients, and pour the soy milk, sour cream and agave into the well.

Combine the wet and dry ingredients with a wooden spoon or rubber spatula. Once everything starts to come together, begin to knead with your hands until the dough forms a ball. If the dough is a little sticky, add about a tablespoon (8 g) of flour at a time until it is no longer sticky. Put the dough in a large bowl that has been sprayed with nonstick spray. Cover the dough with a kitchen towel, and let the dough rest for 1 to 2 hours.

While the dough rests, make the lemon-garlic oil. In a small mixing bowl, whisk together the olive oil, garlic and lemon zest. Set aside.

Make the toppings. Preheat the oven to 400°F (204°C). Put the broccoli florets on a large baking sheet. Drizzle with the olive oil, and sprinkle with a pinch of salt and pepper. Toss to coat. Roast for 10 to 12 minutes, or until the broccoli is tender and starting to brown.

Once the dough has rested and you are ready to make the flatbreads, turn the dough out onto a floured surface, then cut the dough in half, and roll each piece of dough out into a rectangle however thick you want your crust.

Increase the oven temperature to 450°F (232°C).

Place each flatbread onto a baking sheet or pizza pan that has been sprayed with nonstick spray. Brush each flatbread with half of the lemon garlic oil. Spread half the roasted broccoli onto each flatbread. Break apart the bacon into bits, and sprinkle onto each flatbread. Sprinkle half of the mozzarella onto each flatbread, spreading it out evenly. Put half the lemon slices on each flatbread as well.

Bake the flatbread for 10 to 15 minutes, or until the flatbread is golden brown.

While the flatbreads bake, whisk together the agave and hot sauce. Once the flatbreads are done, drizzle them with the spicy agave. Slice and serve.

Sweet Potato Gnocchi with Sage Butter

Whenever I make gnocchi, it's *always* a huge hit. Is it the pillowy perfection of those yummy little dumplings? Is it the savory pasta flavors that pair so well with gnocchi? Is it fun to eat? Yes. All of the above. This recipe is so delicious. Because sweet potatoes are the star of the show, this dish is lighter than using regular potatoes. The fresh sage adds an earthy, peppery flavor to an already bangin' dish. Throw some vegan parmesan on top, and you're ready for an incredible meal.

Serves 6

2 medium sweet potatoes

2 cups (250 g) all-purpose flour, plus more for dusting

2 tsp (12 g) salt

½ cup (108 g) vegan butter

6 cloves garlic, finely chopped

A few pinches of salt and pepper

¼ cup (16 g) fresh sage, chopped

Vegan Parmesan, for topping

Preheat the oven to 400°F (204°C).

Poke holes all over the sweet potatoes with a fork. Place them directly on the oven rack, and bake for 45 to 50 minutes, or until the sweet potatoes are very tender. Remove the sweet potatoes from the oven, and let them cool. You want them cool enough to handle. While the potatoes cool, sift the flour into a large mixing bowl. Stir in the salt. Make a well in the center of the flour.

Once the sweet potatoes have cooled, peel them and grate them into the center of the flour mixture where you made the well. They may be tough to grate because they are soft, but just do the best you can. You want finely grated sweet potatoes. Once all the sweet potatoes have been grated, start to work the sweet potatoes into the flour, and once the dough starts coming together, begin to knead the dough until the flour and sweet potatoes are fully combined. If the dough is still sticky, start adding a little more flour at a time, kneading it into the dough, until the dough is no longer sticky.

Turn the dough out onto a floured surface. Cut the dough in half. Roll each half into a long thin rope, about 1 inch (2.5 cm) in diameter. Now you can cut about 1-inch (2.5-cm) pieces and leave them as is, in about 1 x 1–inch (2.5 x 2.5–cm) squares. Or, you can take those squares and roll them on a gnocchi roller to make the classic lines.

Bring a large pot of salted water to a boil, and add the gnocchi in batches so you don't overcrowd the pot. Simmer for about 2 minutes. The gnocchi will float when they are done. Remove the gnocchi with a slotted spoon. Put them in a bowl, and then repeat until all the gnocchi are done. I like to drizzle a little olive oil over the gnocchi so it doesn't stick together.

In a large nonstick skillet over medium heat, heat the butter. Once the butter is melted, add the garlic. Sauté for 5 to 6 minutes, reducing the heat as needed, or until the butter begins to brown slightly. Add the gnocchi to the skillet, and toss. Sauté, letting the gnocchi get a little brown and crisp on the outside, for 2 to 3 minutes. Season the gnocchi with a few pinches of salt and pepper. Add the fresh sage to the skillet, and toss to combine. Let it simmer for 1 to 2 minutes.

Serve immediately with some Parmesan on top.

Let Them Eat Cake
...IN BED

Desserts, hot or cold, are absolutely comforting. Why? Because so many of our most heart-warming memories revolve around dessert.

The world has been so crazy and filled with uncertainty in the past few years, so why not make one of the desserts in this chapter, put on your robe and hop into bed while you delight in a yummy dessert? Savor every bite in silence, or dive in while you read a book or watch your favorite show. The Gooey Pumpkin Chocolate Chip Cookie Pie (page 173) is an autumn fanatic/cookie lover's dream dessert. The Blackberry-Lavender Sheet Cake (page 170) is a delicious and beautiful work of art. The Funfetti® Cake Ice Cream (page 159) just screams "I'd like to feel like a kid again, please and thank you!"

Feel free to share with a friend or loved one, make and take to a work party, or keep it all for yourself. Your choice, no judgments from me.

Julie's Caramel, Nougat and Peanut Pie

My blog manager (and longtime BFF), Julie's favorite candy bar pre-veganism was a Snickers® bar. So I dedicated this decadent pie to her because it tastes just like a Snickers bar. She absolutely loved it (and still talks about it), and I have no doubt that you will, too. Since it's a candy bar–inspired pie, it would be the perfect dessert for a Halloween party for kids or adults.

Serves 8

Crust

1½ cups (150 g) vegan graham cracker crumbs

¼ cup (55 g) vegan light brown sugar

⅓ cup (72 g) vegan butter, melted

½ cup (73 g) peanuts, chopped

Nougat Layer

¾ cup (109 g) raw cashews, soaked (see Note)

⅓ cup (80 ml) full-fat coconut milk

3 tbsp (40 g) coconut oil, melted

1½ tbsp (23 ml) maple syrup

2 tbsp (26 g) organic cane sugar

1 tsp vanilla extract

⅓ cup (28 g) almond meal

½ cup (120 ml) nondairy milk of choice

Pinch of salt

Caramel Layer

½ cup (120 ml) maple syrup

¼ cup (65 g) peanut butter

½ tsp vanilla extract

¼ tsp salt

½ cup (73 g) peanuts, chopped

Preheat the oven to 350°F (176°C).

Make the crust. In a large mixing bowl, stir together the graham cracker crumbs and brown sugar. Pour in the butter, and stir until fully combined.

Press the graham cracker crumbs down firmly into a 9 inch (23 cm) pie pan evenly. Bake the crust for 10 to 12 minutes, or until the crust is golden brown and firm. Remove the crust from the oven, and sprinkle the chopped peanuts into the crust evenly. Let the crust cool.

While the crust cools, make the nougat. Drain the cashews, and add them to a blender with the coconut milk, coconut oil, maple syrup, cane sugar, vanilla, almond meal, milk and a pinch of salt. Blend on high, scraping down the sides as needed, until the mixture is completely smooth.

Once the crust has cooled, pour the nougat layer into the crust. Smooth it out evenly, and put it in the refrigerator to chill for at least 2 hours, or until the nougat layer is firm.

Make the caramel layer. In a small heat-proof bowl, whisk together the maple syrup, peanut butter, vanilla and salt. Microwave the mixture in 30-second intervals until everything has melted together and the mixture is very hot. I usually only do two intervals.

Pour the hot peanut butter caramel over the nougat layer and smooth out evenly. Sprinkle the top with the chopped peanuts. Put the pie back in the refrigerator, and chill for another hour, or until the caramel layer is firm.

(continued)

Julie's Caramel, Nougat and Peanut Pie (Continued)

Chocolate Layer

1 cup (168 g) vegan dark chocolate chips or chunks

1 tsp solid coconut oil

¼ cup (37 g) peanuts, chopped

Sea salt, for topping

Vegan whipped cream, for topping (optional)

Make the chocolate layer. In a small heat-proof bowl, combine the dark chocolate and coconut oil, and microwave in 30-second intervals, stirring after each interval, until the chocolate has melted. Whisk until smooth.

Drizzle the chocolate on top of the pie in any design you want. Quickly sprinkle with the chopped peanuts and sea salt; the chocolate will firm up fast. Place the pie back in the refrigerator for at least another 1 to 2 hours, or overnight. When you're ready to serve, slice the pie and top with vegan whipped cream, if desired. Keep refrigerated.

Note: You need to soak the cashews in room-temperature water for 8 hours or overnight, or you can boil the cashews for 15 to 20 minutes.

Funfetti® Cake Ice Cream

This ice cream will instantly transport you back to childhood. The Funfetti® cake crumbles are super fun and baked until crunchy. So, let me issue a warning: You may not be able to stop popping these crispy morsels of sprinkle heaven into your mouth. I have been nervous that, in the wake of my unstoppable morsel popping, I wouldn't have enough of the crumbles to add to the ice cream. The ice cream is a very simple vanilla, no-churn ice cream. Which is good news, since you'll want to eat it as soon as possible.

Serves 4

Funfetti Cake Crumbles
¾ cup (155 g) organic cane sugar

2 tbsp (28 g) vegan light brown sugar

1 cup (125 g) all-purpose flour

½ tsp salt

3 tbsp (36 g) vegan rainbow sprinkles (I prefer Sweetapolita™)

½ cup (108 g) room-temperature vegan butter

2 tsp (10 ml) vanilla extract

Ice Cream
2 (13.5-oz [399-ml]) cans coconut cream or full-fat coconut milk, chilled

1 cup (120 g) vegan confectioners' sugar

2 tsp (10 ml) vanilla extract

Pinch of salt

2 tbsp (24 g) rainbow sprinkles

Preheat the oven to 325°F (163°C). Line a large baking dish with parchment paper or a silicone mat.

Make the crumbles. In a large mixing bowl, whisk to combine the cane sugar, brown sugar, flour and salt. Pour in the sprinkles, and stir to combine. Add dollops of the butter all around the bowl. With a fork or your fingers, work the butter into the dry ingredients. Once you have it worked in evenly, pour in the vanilla. Continue to work the vanilla and butter into the dry ingredients until the mixture resembles large crumbles.

Spread the crumbles out evenly on the prepared baking sheet. Bake for about 10 minutes, toss the crumbles, spread them back out and bake for 3 to 6 minutes, or until the crumbles are crunchy and golden brown. They will get crunchier as they cool.

While the crumbles bake, start the ice cream base. In a large mixing bowl or the bowl of a stand mixer, add the chilled coconut cream, just the thick part. Whip the coconut cream with a whisk attachment of a hand mixer or the whisk attachment of a stand mixer. Once it starts to get fluffy, 1 to 2 minutes, start adding the confectioners' sugar a little at a time until it is fully incorporated. Add in the vanilla and a pinch of salt. Continue to whip until the coconut cream is thick and creamy, 1 to 2 more minutes. Fold in the sprinkles.

Pour the ice cream base into a plastic container, or any freezer-safe container you have on hand. Place in the freezer to chill for about 1 hour.

Meanwhile, once the crumbles are done baking, let them cool completely on the counter.

Once the ice cream base has chilled, remove it from the freezer and fold the cooled crumbles into the ice cream. Smooth the ice cream back out. Put back in the freezer for at least 2 to 3 more hours, or until ready to serve.

*See photo on page 161.

Flourless Chocolate-Hazelnut Cake

Oh, man, I love a flourless chocolate cake, and I really wanted to tackle this one and make a vegan version for all us chocolate lovers and for all my gluten-free friends out there. This recipe was a doozy. Since flourless chocolate cake is normally mostly eggs, I had a hard time getting it the way I wanted it. All that work paid off, though, and I'm pretty sure you'll love this Nutella®-inspired cake just as much as I do. It is definitely not made in the traditional way, but is anything I do ever traditional?

Serves 8

2 cups (150 g) ground hazelnuts, divided

¾ cup (153 g) organic cane sugar

¼ cup (32 g) cornstarch

¾ cup (180 ml) coconut milk

¾ cup (180 ml) almond or oat milk

12 oz (340 g) vegan dark chocolate, chopped

Pinch of salt

2 tsp (10 ml) vanilla extract

Vegan whipped topping, for serving

Line an 8-inch (20-cm) cake pan with parchment paper, and then spray the pan with nonstick spray. Sprinkle ½ cup (38 g) of the ground hazelnuts into the bottom of the cake pan, and spread them out evenly.

In a medium saucepan, whisk together the cane sugar and cornstarch until fully combined and there are no lumps of cornstarch left. Pour in the coconut and almond milks. Whisk to combine, again making sure there are no lumps.

Heat the saucepan over medium heat, whisking the milk mixture constantly, and bring to a simmer. Reduce the heat to low, and let the mixture thicken, 2 to 3 minutes. Add in the dark chocolate and a pinch of salt. Whisk until the chocolate has completely melted. The mixture should be nice and thick. Turn off the heat and add the vanilla and 1 cup (75 g) of the ground hazelnuts. Fold together with a rubber spatula.

Pour the chocolate-hazelnut mixture into the cake pan, and smooth out evenly. Top that with the remaining ½ cup (38 g) of ground hazelnuts, and press them down onto the cake. Chill for 4 to 6 hours, or until the cake is completely firm.

When ready to serve, slice and top with vegan whipped topping, if desired.

Coconut Cream Tres Leches Cake

For a long time, I thought I hated coconut. I avoided any desserts with coconut, only thinking of the fake coconutty flavor that I know was in a lot of desserts I was served as a kid. Growing up in the South, my family used a lot of coconut, and it was really played out for me. Once I moved to Miami, I realized how much I actually love all things coconut. This cake is a nod to my teenage years spent in Miami, with all the coconut and all the tres leches.

Serves 12

Cake
1 cup (240 ml) oat milk or other nondairy milk

1 tbsp (15 ml) apple cider vinegar

⅓ cup (72 g) vegan butter, softened

¾ cup (153 g) organic cane sugar

1 tsp vanilla extract

1 tsp coconut extract

1¼ cups (156 g) all-purpose flour

3 tbsp (24 g) cornstarch

1 tsp baking powder

½ tsp baking soda

¼ tsp salt

Milk Mixture
¾ cup (180 ml) coconut milk

⅓ cup (80 ml) almond milk

⅔ cup (160 ml) oat milk

⅓ cup (67 g) organic cane sugar

⅓ cup (73 g) vegan light brown sugar

1 tsp vanilla extract

Pinch of salt

Pinch of cinnamon

Preheat the oven to 350°F (176°C). Line a 9 x 9–inch (23 x 23–cm) baking dish with parchment paper.

Make the cake batter. In a small mixing bowl or a large liquid measuring cup, whisk together the oat milk and apple cider vinegar. Set aside for 2 to 3 minutes. It will start to curdle slightly and make vegan "buttermilk."

In a large mixing bowl or the bowl of a stand mixer, combine the butter and cane sugar. Begin to beat together, either with a hand mixer or the paddle attachment of a stand mixer. Beat until fully combined and the mixture is light and fluffy. Add the vanilla and coconut extract, and beat for another minute just to combine.

In a separate mixing bowl, sift together the flour, cornstarch, baking powder and baking soda. Stir in the salt. Add the dry ingredients to the butter and sugar mixture, a little at a time, alternating with the oat milk mixture, beating to combine until everything is fully incorporated.

Pour the batter into the prepared baking dish. Smooth out evenly with a rubber spatula. Bake for 30 to 32 minutes, or until a toothpick comes out clean from the center of the cake.

While the cake bakes, make the milk mixture. In a medium saucepan, whisk together the coconut milk, almond milk, oat milk, cane sugar, brown sugar, vanilla and a pinch each of salt and cinnamon. Heat the saucepan over medium heat, bring to a simmer, reduce the heat to low and let it simmer, whisking frequently, until the sugars dissolve and the mixture thickens slightly, 5 to 7 minutes.

Once the cake is done, remove the cake from the oven, and poke holes all over the cake with a knife. Pour the milk mixture all over the top of the cake, letting it absorb. Let the cake cool on the counter for 15 to 20 minutes, then put it in the refrigerator, and let the cake chill and absorb all of the liquid for 6 hours or overnight.

(continued)

Coconut Cream Tres Leches Cake (Continued)

Topping

1 (13.5-oz [399-ml]) can full-fat coconut milk or coconut cream, chilled

½ cup (60 g) vegan confectioners' sugar

1 tsp vanilla extract

1 cup (93 g) coconut flakes, toasted

When ready to serve the cake, make the coconut cream topping. In a large mixing bowl or the bowl of a stand mixer, add the chilled coconut milk, just the thick part. Whip the coconut milk with the whisk attachment for a hand mixer or the stand mixer. Once it starts to get fluffy, add the confectioners' sugar a little at a time until it is fully incorporated. Add the vanilla, and continue to whip for another 1 to 2 minutes.

Top the cake with the coconut whipped cream, smoothing it out evenly with a rubber spatula. Top that with the toasted coconut. Cut into squares and serve.

Betwixt Bars

I LOVED Twix® bars when I was a kid. I would have sold my soul for one (I played it pretty fast and loose with my soul possession from the ages of eight to fifteen). These days, when I need my Twix fix, these are where it's at.

Yields 12 bars

Shortbread Layer
1¼ cups (156 g) all-purpose flour

¼ cup (51 g) organic cane sugar

Pinch of salt

⅔ cup (151 g) room-temperature vegan butter

Caramel Layer
½ cup (108 g) vegan butter

½ cup (102 g) organic cane sugar

½ cup (110 g) vegan light brown sugar

⅓ cup (80 ml) coconut cream or full-fat coconut milk

½ cup (120 ml) maple syrup

1 tsp vanilla extract

Pinch of salt

Chocolate Layer
1½ cups (252 g) vegan dark chocolate chips

1 tsp solid coconut oil

Sea salt, for topping (optional)

Preheat the oven to 350°F (176°C). Line an 8 x 8–inch (20 x 20–cm) baking dish with parchment paper.

Make the shortbread layer. In a large bowl, whisk together the flour, cane sugar and a pinch of salt. Break the butter into small pieces, and drop them into the dry mixture. Using a fork, cut the butter into the dry mixture until it is crumbly. Using your hands, make sure there are no large lumps of butter and that it is distributed evenly. Pour the mixture into the prepared baking dish, and press the shortbread crust down evenly in the pan with your hands. Poke some holes in the top of the shortbread with a fork, and bake for 18 to 20 minutes, or until the shortbread looks firm.

While the shortbread bakes, make the caramel layer. In a medium saucepan over medium heat, add the butter. Once the butter is melted, whisk in the cane sugar and brown sugar. Make sure it is fully incorporated and melts into the butter. Whisk in the coconut cream, maple syrup, vanilla and a pinch of salt. Whisk until fully combined.

Attach a candy thermometer to the side of the pan, making sure it isn't touching the bottom of the pan. Bring the caramel mixture to a simmer, and reduce the heat to medium-low, reducing the heat more as needed, and simmer the mixture, without whisking, until it reaches 235°F (113°C) or the soft ball stage, about 15 minutes. Keep your eyes on it, as it can burn easily. Once the temperature reaches 235°F (113°C), remove the saucepan from the heat, and let it cool for 5 to 10 minutes. It will start to thicken.

When the shortbread layer is done, let it cool for 10 to 15 minutes. Pour the caramel over the top of the shortbread layer, and spread it out evenly with a rubber spatula. Let it cool completely on the counter for about 30 minutes, then put it in the refrigerator for 1 to 2 hours.

Make the chocolate layer. In a heat-proof bowl, add the chocolate chips and microwave in 30-second intervals, stirring after each interval with a rubber spatula, until the chocolate is melted. Add the coconut oil to the melted chocolate, and stir to combine. Pour the chocolate over the caramel layer, and smooth out evenly. Sprinkle with sea salt, if desired, and put it back in the refrigerator to completely set, at least 2 hours or up to overnight.

When ready to serve, cut it into squares.

*See photo on page 167.

Peanut Butter Cookies and Cream Milkshake

My third trimester of pregnancy brought the onset of my milkshake cravings. Hard-freaking-core. I was throwing this into the blender, I was throwing that into the blender. I made some crazy concoctions, many involving full slices of cake or pie. However, none were more inviting, or satisfied my cravings better, than this recipe. The combination of peanut butter and chocolate cookies is the milkshake we all need, we all want and everything we deserve.

Serves 2 to 4

1 cup (240 ml) oat milk or other nondairy milk

3 cups (450 g) vegan vanilla ice cream

⅓ cup (86 g) peanut butter

1 tsp vanilla extract

8 chocolate sandwich cookies (I prefer Joe-Joe's)

Vegan whipped cream, for topping (optional)

In a blender, combine the oat milk, ice cream, peanut butter, vanilla and chocolate sandwich cookies. Blend on high until completely smooth, 1 to 2 minutes. Serve immediately with vegan whipped cream, if desired.

Guava Cream Cheeze Cupcakes

Delightfully tropical and refreshing, these fruity cupcakes are a dessert lover's dream. On the surface these might seem like basic vanilla cake cupcakes, but surprise! There's a yummy whipped guava paste in the center of these moist, fluffy gems. As a little guava bonus, there's also guava paste in the sweet cream cheeze frosting. These babies are also kid-tested and kid-approved. Bake these crowd-pleasing cupcakes for your child's poolside birthday party, or for your midsummer cookout. Plan to bake extra since it's impossible to just eat one.

Yields 16 to 18 cupcakes

Cupcakes

1⅔ cups (208 g) all-purpose flour

1 cup (200 g) organic cane sugar

1½ tsp (7 g) baking powder

½ tsp baking soda

1 tsp salt

¾ cup (185 g) room-temperature vegan butter

½ cup (120 ml) aquafaba (liquid from a can of chickpeas)

1 tbsp (15 ml) vanilla extract

1 cup plus 2 tbsp (270 ml) oat milk or other nondairy milk, divided

½ cup (160 g) guava paste

Frosting

2 tbsp (28 g) room-temperature vegan butter

2 tbsp (19 g) vegetable shortening

8 oz (226 g) vegan cream cheese (I prefer Violife)

3 tbsp (60 g) guava paste

2 tsp (10 ml) vanilla extract

3½ cups (420 g) vegan confectioners' sugar

Pinch of salt

Preheat the oven to 350°F (176°C).

Make the cupcakes. In a large mixing bowl, sift the flour. Whisk in the cane sugar, baking powder, baking soda and salt. Set aside.

In a separate large mixing bowl or the bowl of a stand mixer, add the butter, aquafaba and vanilla. Using the paddle attachment for the stand mixer or a hand mixer, begin to beat together for 2 to 3 minutes. It will not fully come together, but mix as well as you can. Add the dry ingredients to the wet about ½ cup (60 g) at a time, alternating with 1 cup (240 ml) of the oat milk, beating together until everything is fully combined.

Put cupcake liners into a cupcake pan, and then fill each liner up about three-quarters of the way. Set aside.

Make the guava filling. In a clean mixing bowl, add the guava paste and the remaining 2 tablespoons (30 ml) of oat milk. Whip together for 2 to 3 minutes, or until smooth and creamy. You may still have a few chunks left.

Put about 1 teaspoon of the whipped guava into the center of each cupcake. Just right on top; the guava will sink in slightly and be at the center of the cupcake once baked. Bake for 18 to 20 minutes, or until a toothpick comes out clean from the cake portion of the cupcake.

Let the cupcakes cool completely, then make the frosting. In a large mixing bowl or the bowl of a stand mixer, whip together the butter and vegetable shortening until fully combined. Add in the cream cheese, guava paste and vanilla, and continue to whip until combined, about 2 minutes. Add the confectioners' sugar, about ½ cup (60 g) at a time, whipping together until fully combined and the frosting is light and fluffy. Add a pinch of salt, and whip again to combine.

Frost the cupcakes, either with a piping bag or a rubber spatula. Decorate with more guava on top, if desired. Keep chilled until ready to serve.

Blackberry-Lavender Sheet Cake

You'll be so proud to share this gorgeous sheet cake with your friends and family. Blackberry-lavender jam not only appears in the cake itself, but is creatively swirled throughout a classic vanilla frosting. It is great for celebratory get togethers, or for sad and gloomy office parties when something cheerful is necessary.

Serves 12

Blackberry-Lavender Jam
5 cups (720 g) fresh blackberries

⅓ cup (80 ml) light agave syrup

2 tsp (10 ml) lemon juice

1 tbsp (6 g) dried lavender

Cake
3 cups (360 g) cake flour

1 tsp baking powder

½ tsp baking soda

1½ cups (302 g) organic cane sugar

½ tsp salt

1 cup (220 g) vegan butter, room-temperature

2 tsp (10 ml) vanilla extract

1⅓ cups (320 ml) oat milk or other nondairy milk, divided

2 tbsp (14 g) flax meal

3 tbsp (45 ml) water

½ cup (120 ml) applesauce

Frosting
½ cup (108 g) room-temperature vegan butter

½ cup (95 g) vegetable shortening

3 cups (360 g) vegan confectioners' sugar

1 tsp vanilla extract

Pinch of salt

Make the blackberry-lavender jam. In a medium saucepan, add the blackberries, agave, lemon juice and lavender. Stir to combine. Heat the saucepan over medium-high heat. Bring the jam to a simmer, reduce the heat to low and simmer for 10 to 12 minutes, or until the berries have broken down and start to thicken. Mash the blackberries with a fork or potato masher. Remove the jam from the heat to cool completely.

Preheat the oven to 350°F (176°C). Grease a 9 x 13–inch (23 x 33–cm) baking dish or line with parchment paper.

In a large mixing bowl or the bowl of a stand mixer, sift together the cake flour, baking powder and baking soda. Stir in the cane sugar and salt. Add the butter, vanilla and ⅓ cup (80 ml) of the oat milk to the dry ingredients, and beat, using a hand mixer or the paddle attachment of a stand mixer, for about 1 minute, or until the dry ingredients are moist. Set aside.

Make a flax egg. In a small mixing bowl, whisk together the flax meal and water until combined. Let it sit for 3 to 5 minutes to thicken. Add the flax egg, applesauce and remaining 1 cup (240 ml) of oat milk to the bowl with the batter, and continue to beat until everything is smooth and fully combined, 1 to 2 minutes, making sure not to over mix.

Pour the batter into the prepared baking dish. Spread it out evenly with a rubber spatula. Drop large dollops, 1 to 2 tablespoons (15 to 30 ml) each, of the jam all over the top of the cake batter. You should use about half the jam, reserving the rest for the frosting. Using a knife, swirl the jam into the batter. Bake for 35 to 38 minutes, or until a toothpick comes out of the center clean. Let it cool completely.

Make the frosting. In a large mixing bowl or the bowl of a stand mixer, add the butter and vegetable shortening. Beat together, with a hand mixer or the paddle attachment of a stand mixer, until light and fluffy, about 1 minute. Add the confectioners' sugar, 1 cup (120 g) at a time, until it is fully blended and the frosting is nice and thick. Add the vanilla and a pinch of salt. Blend again for about 30 seconds.

When the cake is completely cool, frost the top of the cake evenly with the vanilla frosting. Take the remaining jam and put dollops on top of the frosting. Swirl the jam into the frosting with a knife. Cut into squares and serve.

Gooey Pumpkin Chocolate Chip Cookie Pie

If you tell me a restaurant has any kind of vegan autumnal-flavored desserts, just give me 15 minutes and I'll be there. I know, I know. Pumpkin flavors have gotten a bad rap. They're "basic." A flavor adored by the soccer moms out there. Well, this cookie pie is anything but basic. The center is ooey and gooey. The pumpkin goes so well with the melty dark chocolate. Plus, this cookie pie is actually baked in the perfect buttery, flaky crust. Serve it warm with ice cream and *boom*. It's better than any dessert at any restaurant.

Serves 8

Crust

1¼ cups (185 g) all purpose flour, plus more for dusting

1 tsp organic cane sugar

½ tsp ground cinnamon

¼ tsp salt

4 tbsp (54 g) cold vegan butter

4 tbsp (54 g) solid coconut oil

4 tbsp (60 ml) cold water

Filling

½ cup (113 g) canned pumpkin puree

½ cup (63 g) all-purpose flour

½ cup (102 g) organic cane sugar

½ cup (110 g) vegan light brown sugar

1 tsp ground cinnamon

½ tsp nutmeg

½ tsp salt

1 tsp vanilla extract

¾ cup (185 g) room-temperature vegan butter

1 cup (180 g) vegan chocolate chips

Preheat the oven to 325°F (163°C).

Make the crust. In a food processor, add the flour, cane sugar, cinnamon and salt. Pulse once or twice to mix.

Cut the butter into cubes, and drop them into the food processor. Then drop dollops of the coconut oil into the food processor. Pulse again for about a minute, or until the butter and coconut oil are mixed in evenly and the mixture resembles sand.

While the food processor is running, drizzle in the cold water. The dough should come together and form a ball.

Put the dough ball on a floured surface, and flatten it out slightly. Sprinkle a little flour on the top of the dough and, using a rolling pin, roll it out, starting from the center and working your way out, until it is ⅛ inch (3 mm) thick and slightly wider than your pie pan.

I like to fold my pie crust over my rolling pin to help lay it in the pie pan. Lay your pie crust into a 9-inch (23-cm) pie pan, press it down, then trim the edges. Poke a few holes in the bottom of the pie crust with a fork, then set aside.

Make the filling. In a large mixing bowl or the bowl of a stand mixer, combine the pumpkin puree, flour, cane sugar, brown sugar, cinnamon, nutmeg and salt. Using a hand mixer or the paddle attachment for a stand mixer, beat the mixture until everything is fully combined, about 1 minute.

Add the vanilla and butter to the mixing bowl, and continue to beat until fully combined, another 1 to 2 minutes, scraping down the sides as needed. Pour the chocolate chips into the mixing bowl, and fold them in.

Pour the filling into the uncooked pie crust, smooth out evenly with a rubber spatula and bake for 55 to 57 minutes. The filling will still look a little jiggly, but will firm once cooled. Just make sure the crust is cooked through and the cookie filling is browned.

Let it cool completely for 1 to 2 hours, cut into slices and serve with vegan ice cream, if desired.

Strawberry-Basil Shortcake

There's just something about shortcake, isn't there? Maybe it's the crumbly, crisp texture. Or maybe it's the strawberry juices mixing with the crumbling texture. All I know is that shortcake is delicious, it's been around for a long time and most people have a nostalgic tie to it.

This Strawberry-Basil Shortcake takes a classic, beloved recipe and kicks it up a notch. The compote features the usual strawberries, but the strawberries brought their friend basil over to play. You will love this strawberry-basil combo. It's unique and the basil enhances the delicious berry flavor. They really do play well together.

Serves 8

Strawberry-Basil Compote
3 cups (432 g) strawberries, halved or quartered

1 tbsp (15 ml) lemon juice

3 tbsp (39 g) organic cane sugar

¼ cup (10 g) fresh basil, chopped

Shortcakes
4 cups (500 g) all-purpose flour, plus more for dusting

¼ cup (51 g) organic cane sugar

¾ tsp salt

5 tsp (23 g) baking powder

¾ cup (185 g) cold vegan butter

1¼ cups (300 ml) oat milk or other nondairy milk

1 tsp vanilla extract

Oil, vegan butter or nonstick spray, for brushing

For Serving (Optional)
Vegan whipped topping

Vegan ice cream

Make the compote. In a medium saucepan, combine the strawberries, lemon juice and sugar. Stir to combine, and let the strawberries sit for about 5 minutes. They will start to release their juices.

Heat the saucepan over medium heat, and bring to a simmer. Reduce the heat to low, and let the strawberries simmer for about 10 minutes, stirring every few minutes. The strawberries should start to break down, and the juices should thicken slightly. Remove from the heat, stir in the basil and let it cool.

Make the shortcakes. Preheat the oven to 450°F (232°C). Line a large baking sheet with parchment paper or spray with nonstick spray.

In a large mixing bowl, whisk together the flour, sugar, salt and baking powder. Cut the cold butter into cubes, and add them to the dry ingredients. Press and pinch the butter into the dry ingredients with a fork, pastry cutter or just your fingers, until the butter is evenly distributed and the dry ingredients resemble sand.

Pour the oat milk and vanilla into the bowl, and stir until fully combined. Your dough should be thick but no longer sticky. Turn the dough out onto a floured surface, and fold your dough over itself a few times. Roll the dough out with a rolling pin so it is ½ to ¾ inch (1.3 to 2 cm) thick.

Cut out circles using a biscuit cutter or a cup. Once you make as many as you can on the first roll out, bring together the dough scraps, roll back out, and make more circles.

Place the shortcakes on the prepared baking sheet. Brush the tops with oil or butter or spray with nonstick spray. Bake for 10 to 15 minutes, or until they are light brown and firm.

To serve, let the shortcakes cool slightly, cut them in half and top with some of the strawberry-basil compote and vegan whipped topping or ice cream, if desired.

Banana Bread Cobbler

A fun and unique take on a classic cobbler, this dessert might change your whole existence. Dive into a buttery, cinnamon and nutmeg–spiced cobbler, with a layer of sliced bananas on top. The final layer is a delicious caramelized oat and pecan crumble. The combination of banana bread and cobbler is divine. Top it with some vegan ice cream, and you're all set.

Serves 9

Base

1 cup (125 g) all-purpose flour

1½ tsp (7 g) baking powder

1 cup (200 g) organic cane sugar

1 tsp ground cinnamon

¼ tsp nutmeg

½ tsp salt

1 cup (240 ml) soy milk or other nondairy milk

½ cup (108 g) room-temperature vegan butter

1 tsp vanilla extract

3 large bananas, sliced

Topping

¾ cup (165 g) vegan light brown sugar

½ cup (63 g) all-purpose flour

¾ tsp baking powder

1 cup (90 g) quick-cooking oats

1 tsp ground cinnamon

¼ tsp salt

½ cup (55 g) roasted pecans, chopped

½ cup (108 g) room-temperature coconut oil or vegan butter

Vegan ice cream, for serving (optional)

Preheat the oven to 375°F (190°C). Grease an 8 x 8– or 9 x 9–inch (20 x 20– or 23 x 23–cm) baking dish with butter or nonstick spray.

Make the base. In a large mixing bowl or the bowl of a stand mixer, sift the flour and baking powder. Stir in the cane sugar, cinnamon, nutmeg and salt. Whisk to combine.

Using the paddle attachment of a stand mixer or a hand mixer, slowly add the soy milk to the dry ingredients, beating together the whole time. Add the butter and vanilla. Continue beating the batter together until fully combined, 1 to 2 minutes. There may be a few lumps of butter; that's fine.

Pour the batter into the prepared baking dish. Smooth it out evenly with a rubber spatula. Spread the sliced bananas out evenly on top of the batter.

Make the topping. In a large mixing bowl, combine the brown sugar, flour, baking powder, oats, cinnamon, salt and pecans. Add the coconut oil or butter and, using a fork or your fingers, press and pinch the oil or butter into the dry ingredients until it has a crumbly texture. It should hold together if you pinch it but be in large pieces.

Spread the crumble over the bananas in the baking dish. Spread it out evenly with a rubber spatula. Bake for 45 to 50 minutes, or until a toothpick comes out clean.

Serve with vegan ice cream, if desired. I like to serve the cobbler warm.

Porter's Salted Crème Brûlée White Hot Chocolate

This is not your average instant hot chocolate. In case you missed it, Julie is my blog manager and longtime best friend, and her son, Porter, has a serious sweet tooth and loves hot chocolate. I mean, who can blame him? This recipe is the absolute perfect marriage of hot chocolate and crème brûlée. It's for those who intentionally savor every single bite of their dessert. It's a drink for the person who not only tolerates but *delights* in acquiring a fancy whipped cream mustache. This is made for decadent dessert-loving human beings, just like Porter. For the adults, feel free to add coffee for an after-dinner café noir vibe, or make it boozy by adding Kahlúa. No matter how you drink this hot chocolate, you and your guests will gush over how delicious it is.

Serves 4

Sugar Topping
1 cup (200 g) organic cane sugar

½ tsp lemon juice

1 tsp sea salt

Hot Chocolate
2 cups (480 ml) oat milk or other nondairy milk

1 cup (240 ml) canned coconut cream

2 tbsp (28 g) vegan light brown sugar

1 tbsp (13 g) vanilla bean paste

1 tsp vanilla extract

8 oz (226 g) vegan white chocolate

¼ tsp salt

Vegan whipped cream, for topping

Make the sugar topping. In a small saucepan, whisk together the sugar and lemon juice. Just make sure the lemon juice is evenly distributed and the sugar looks moist. Heat the saucepan over medium-high heat, and stir the sugar with a rubber spatula consistently until the sugar has melted. Reduce the heat to medium-low, and let the sugar simmer very briefly or until all of it has melted and is completely smooth. If you have a candy thermometer, you want the sugar to reach about 240°F (115°C). Remove the sugar from the heat immediately, and pour it onto a silicone mat or parchment paper.

Smooth the caramelized sugar out evenly, and then sprinkle the top of the sugar with the salt. Then let it cool until the caramelized sugar hardens. Once the sugar hardens, you can crack it into small pieces, and leave it on the silicone mat or parchment paper while you make the hot chocolate.

Make the hot chocolate. In a medium saucepan, whisk together the oat milk, coconut cream, brown sugar, vanilla bean paste and vanilla extract.

Heat the saucepan over medium heat, then add the white chocolate and salt. Whisk consistently until the white chocolate has melted, 2 to 3 minutes. Reduce the heat to low, and let it simmer for about 2 minutes. Turn off the heat.

Pour the hot chocolate into cups, top with vegan whipped cream, if desired, and sprinkle the caramelized sugar crumbs on top of the whipped cream. Serve immediately.

Mixed Berry Lemonade Pie Bars

These berry lemonade bars taste like summer. Like sitting on the porch, sipping lemonade, gossiping with friends, just enjoying life. But don't take my word for it, mostly because I have literally never done that. I lived in Florida for most of my summers, so if I even attempted to do that, mosquitos would eat me alive. And now that I live in Nevada, well, let's just say it was 110°F (43°C) outside yesterday. So, if you're in the same boat as me, just make these incredible, sweet and tangy dessert bars, and really experience the summers you've been dreaming of.

Serves 12

Crust

2½ cups (300 g) vegan graham cracker crumbs

3 tbsp (42 g) organic cane sugar

¾ cup (185 g) vegan butter, melted

Filling

1 cup (200 g) organic cane sugar

⅓ cup (30 g) berry powder (see Note)

6 tbsp (48 g) cornstarch

1 cup (240 ml) lemon juice

1 cup (240 ml) canned coconut milk

1½ cups (360 ml) oat milk

1 tsp lemon zest

Pinch of salt

Vegan whipped topping (optional)

Preheat the oven to 350°F (176°C).

Make the crust. In a large mixing bowl, combine the graham cracker crumbs, cane sugar and butter. Stir to combine and evenly distribute the butter.

Press the graham cracker crumbs into a 9 x 13–inch (23 x 33–cm) baking dish. Press the crumbs down evenly with a cup or your hand. Bake for 12 to 14 minutes, or until the crust is looking golden brown and firm. Let the crust cool.

Make the filling. In a medium saucepan, whisk together the cane sugar, berry powder and cornstarch. Whisk until there are no lumps of cornstarch left.

Pour in the lemon juice, coconut milk and oat milk. Heat the saucepan over medium-high heat. Bring to a simmer, then reduce the heat to low. Add the lemon zest and a pinch of salt, then whisk to combine. Continue whisking frequently until the filling is very thick and coats the back of a spoon, 3 to 5 minutes.

Pour the filling over the crust, then smooth it out evenly with a rubber spatula. Let it cool on the counter for 20 to 30 minutes. Put it in the refrigerator for 4 to 6 hours, or until the filling is completely set and firm.

When you're ready to serve, cut the pie into bars, and serve with vegan whipped topping, if desired.

Note: Make berry powder by adding freeze-dried blueberries, strawberries and raspberries to a blender or food processor and pulsing until they turn into a powder.

Cookies and (S)cream Cheezecake

Not only is this cheezecake creamy and delicious, it will fool anyone into thinking they are eating a traditional cheesecake. I served this to some non-vegan friends, and they said it tasted exactly like regular cheesecake. They could not believe that I pulled off something so close to the "real" thing. I named this Cookies and (S)cream Cheezecake because I wanted to make a fun Halloween-themed dessert, but this can be made any time of year—just choose a different food coloring. It's velvety-smooth with a yummy cookie-crunch. Seriously, you just have to try this.

Serves 12

Crust
3 cups (260 g) vegan chocolate sandwich cookie crumbs

3 tbsp (42 g) vegan butter, melted

Filling
1 (15-oz [425-g]) block firm tofu

16 oz (454 g) vegan cream cheese

1 cup (200 g) organic cane sugar

½ cup (120 ml) maple syrup

1 tbsp (15 ml) vanilla extract

1 tbsp (8 g) cornstarch

⅓ cup (41 g) all-purpose flour

¾ cup (180 ml) oat milk or other nondairy milk, plus more as needed

Orange food coloring (optional; use as much as needed to reach your desired color)

1 cup (90 g) crushed vegan chocolate sandwich cookies

Vegan whipped topping (optional)

Preheat the oven to 350°F (176°C).

Make the crust. In a large mixing bowl, combine the chocolate cookie crumbs and butter. Stir together with a rubber spatula until everything is combined and the cookie crumbs are moist.

Press the cookie crumbs with your hand or a cup into a 9-inch (23-cm) springform pan, evenly distributing them. Bake the crust for 5 minutes. Remove the crust from the oven, and set it aside while you make the cheezecake filling.

Increase the oven temperature to 375°F (190°C).

Make the filling. Drain and lightly squeeze some of the liquid out of the tofu over the sink.

In a blender, add the tofu, cream cheese, sugar, maple syrup, vanilla, cornstarch, flour and oat milk. Blend on high until the mixture is completely smooth, 2 to 3 minutes. You may need to add a little extra oat milk to help blend it. Just add a little at a time until the mixture is blending easily. Add the food coloring, if using, and blend again for about 30 seconds to reach your desired color.

Stir the crushed chocolate sandwich cookies into the filling. Pour the filling into the springform pan over the crust. Smooth the filling out evenly with a rubber spatula. Place the springform pan on a large baking sheet to catch any leakage.

Bake the cheesecake for 40 to 45 minutes, or until the edges are getting firm. The center will still be a little jiggly. Let it cool completely, 4 to 6 hours or overnight.

Take off the outer ring of the springform pan, slice the cheesecake and serve with vegan whipped topping, if desired.

Carrot Cake Sticky Toffee Pudding

I awoke with a jolt one morning. The reason? In my mind, sticky toffee pudding and carrot cake should become one. It makes so much friggin' sense. They have a lot of the same ingredients, but when I tell you adding carrots to a sticky toffee pudding was a good idea, I am vastly understating what is happening here. The marriage of dates and carrots with the toffee sauce will forever be burned into my brain as one of the best desserts I have ever had.

Serves 6

Cake

7 oz (198 g) Medjool dates, pitted

¾ cup (180 ml) boiling water

1 tsp baking soda

5 tbsp (70 g) room-temperature vegan butter

2 tbsp (30 ml) molasses

⅓ cup (73 g) vegan light brown sugar

½ cup (120 ml) applesauce

1 tsp vanilla extract

½ cup (55 g) shredded carrots

1¼ cups (156 g) all-purpose flour

1 tsp baking powder

1 tsp ground cinnamon

½ tsp dried ginger

¼ tsp nutmeg

¼ tsp salt

Put the dates into a medium heat-proof bowl. Pour the boiling water over the top of the dates. Sprinkle the baking soda over the top of the dates and water. Stir to combine. Let the dates sit submerged in the water for at least 20 minutes.

Preheat the oven to 350°F (176°C). Spray six 8-ounce (237-ml) ramekins with nonstick spray. You can also use a 6-tin muffin pan.

Make the cake. In a large mixing bowl or the bowl of a stand mixer, add the butter, molasses and brown sugar. Beat together, using a hand mixer or the paddle attachment of a stand mixer, until it is fully combined and fluffy, 1 to 2 minutes.

Add the applesauce and vanilla to the bowl. Continue to beat until combined. The mixture will look broken; that is normal. Fold the carrots into the wet mixture. Set aside.

In a separate medium mixing bowl, sift together the flour, baking powder, cinnamon, ginger, nutmeg and salt.

Add the dry ingredients to the wet ingredients, about ½ cup (60 g) at a time, continuing to beat together until it is fully combined, scraping down the sides with a rubber spatula as needed. Don't over mix. Set aside.

Pour the dates and the liquid they have been soaking in into a food processor. Process until the dates become a smooth paste, 1 to 2 minutes. Scoop the date paste into the bowl with the batter, and beat together one more time until the date paste has been fully incorporated.

Pour the batter evenly into the prepared ramekins. Bake for 22 to 27 minutes, or until a toothpick comes out clean from the center of the puddings.

(continued)

Toffee Sauce

½ cup (108 g) vegan butter

¾ cup (180 ml) coconut cream or full-fat coconut milk

¾ cup (165 g) vegan light brown sugar

½ tsp vanilla extract

½ tsp ground cinnamon

Pinch of salt

For Serving (Optional)

Vegan vanilla ice cream

Vegan whipped topping

While the puddings bake, make the toffee sauce. In a small saucepan, add the butter, coconut cream, brown sugar, vanilla, cinnamon and a pinch of salt. Heat the saucepan over medium heat, and begin to whisk everything together.

As the butter melts, continue to whisk until everything has melted together and is fully combined. Bring the mixture to a simmer. Reduce the heat to low, and simmer for 5 to 6 minutes, making sure it stays at a small bubble. It will thicken slightly. Remove from the heat, and let it cool as the puddings finish baking.

Once the puddings are done, let them cool for a few minutes, then loosen them from the ramekins by running a small knife around the edges of the puddings. Invert onto a cooling rack. Let them cool for a few more minutes. Then, while they are still slightly warm, generously brush the tops and the sides of the puddings with the toffee sauce. I like to put a silicone mat under the cooling rack to catch any dripping toffee sauce. You should have plenty of the toffee sauce left for serving.

When ready to serve, put one of the puddings on a plate, drizzle with extra toffee sauce, and serve with vegan vanilla ice cream or vegan whipped cream, if desired.

Acknowledgments

Julie, my platonic life mate:
If you don't know Julie, she has not only helped me run my blog for about 5 years, she has been my friend for about 13 years. We have been through some things together. We have held on to each other, held each other up, talked each other off our respective ledges and been each other's steadfast cheerleaders. I couldn't ask for a better friend or a better person to absolutely laugh my ass off with on any occasion (appropriate or not). Let me tell you, we wrote some ridiculous things into the intros of all these recipes, died of laughter and then tried to make them slightly more appropriate. She not only helped with a lot of the writing of intros for the book, she did a lot of the gorgeous photos you see. I'll be honest, they are probably the photos in this book you like most. To be her best friend makes you the luckiest person in the world, so I guess I'm the luckiest person in the world.

Terry, my non-platonic life mate:
Oh Terry, where do I start? We grew up together in a sense. He went to my culinary school interview with me for goodness sake. We were apart for years and somehow found our way back to each other, and I'm so incredibly grateful. I have yet to meet his match. There just isn't anyone quite like him. He is honest, kind, generous, supportive, brilliant and incredibly funny. Whether he was telling me "everything is going to be okay" or listening to me complain for literally hours at a time, he did it all gracefully and without ever making me feel like I was irritating him. This cookbook was a lot of work; he gave me space when I needed it and held me when I needed holding. He is the absolute best person, and I love him beyond measure.

Ethan, my brother:
I may have a small family, because they are the family I have chosen. But my brother, Ethan, has spent his entire life making sure I never feel alone. Only 2½ years older than me, he has always been there when I needed him. He's my biggest supporter and I am his. He may be the only person on the planet I think I 100 percent just get. Call it genetics or call it luck. However you look at it, I lucked out with him as my brother. We may have had it rough as kids, but when I think about him, it makes me happy. Ethan is so brilliant, kind, understanding and loving. Plus, he is just plain fun to be around.

Lenore, my daughter:
My little Lenny bean. My bean sprout. I gave birth to the love of my life, and I wake up every day and try to make her proud. She loves to try my recipes, and she is so excited when she gets to help with recipe videos. She loves to tell everyone she knows that "her mom is a famous chef." She is uniquely herself, with a humor beyond her years and wit that is unmatched. She is loving, knows exactly what she wants and will not give up until she makes it happen. Lenore is a good friend and a friend to all. She is the reason I work my ass off. She is an avid food lover, like her mom, and we have the best time eating together, gossiping while building LEGO®s and just snuggling together. I love you, baby bean!

Ken, my dad:
I think my dad knew, right from the beginning, that I was different. That I would most likely follow a different path. That I would carve out my own slice of the world, that I would make it uniquely mine and thrive doing it. He never questioned me, he trusted me to find my way. My dad never made me feel like a failure, no matter how many times I got knocked down, because he is also very uniquely himself. He has carved his own path through the mountains. He is brilliant and caring, loving and trustworthy. He and Ethan are the reasons why I'm doing OK. They've loved me unconditionally and I them. I think if I had been raised by any other man, I would not have had the tenacity to make my life what I wanted it to be. His contribution to that is not lost on me, and I am infinitely grateful for his love and support and him just being exactly who he is.

About the Author

Lauren Boehme founded the successful vegan food blog Rabbit and Wolves in 2016.

A talented recipe developer and food photographer, she and the blog continue to gain popularity year after year. Her favorite pastimes when she's not dreaming up delicious plant-based recipes include listening to true-crime podcasts, reading, walking, watching horror movies and laughing with her longtime best friend, blog manager and second photographer, Julie.

A classically trained pastry chef and lover of comfort food, she chooses veganism because she is passionate about not eating animals. However, you won't catch her preaching about veganism. Her goal is not to convert others into a plant-based lifestyle, but to provide delicious recipes for those that want to incorporate more vegan food into their life. Not a full-time vegan? No problem. You'll find amazing dishes to make for your meatless Monday. Nothing makes Lauren happier than to hear from her readers that her unique recipes make going vegan that much easier, or that someone's entire meat-eating family enjoyed one of her popular dishes.

PTSD is a very real part of Lauren's life, and over the last twenty years, cooking and recipe development has become a therapeutic and inspiring activity for her. Sharing her recipes with the world is a gift she does not take for granted. Lauren resides in Las Vegas, Nevada, with her vivacious daughter, Lenore, and her partner, Terry.

Index